AF295473

To my beloved child, without you there would be no me. I love you endlessly.

To my father and my sister Sandra, I love you and miss you every day.

Elin, Ariola and Jasko, your friendship and kindness means the world to me.

Annie Törnroos

GROWING ALONG THE WAY

Illustration: Annie Törnroos. Image from www.pexels.com

Korrekturläsning: Annie Törnroos

Förlag: BoD · Books on Demand, Östermalmstorg 1, 114 42
Stockholm, Sverige, bod@bod.se
Tryck: Libri Plureos GmbH, Friedensallee 273, 22763 Hamburg,
Tyskland

ISBN: 978-91-8080-902-3

Healing also means taking a look at the role you play in your own suffering

- Jay Shetty

-

"Life falls apart, not because the Lord is punishing us for something we did or didn't do. Life falls apart because it needs to break. Life falls apart because the foundation was unstable in the beginning."

- Iyanla Vanzant

This story, my story, involves other people. But those "other people" don't really have much to do with my story. They were there, of course. They influenced things and people. However, this story is based upon my view of what occurred, and someone's story can never be the same for two people, even if they witness the same event. This is because we all interpret the world out of our own thoughts, beliefs, values, and emotions.

Even when several people share a common event, the interpretation of this event will be different for everyone. This means, that just because some people are mentioned in this book, this story, doesn't mean that they share my point of view. It doesn't mean that they personally have anything to do with what I will share with you. They have their own memories and interpretation of what happened, and it's their fully right to have that, as I have mine. This story is not meant to be taken as an absolute fact, where all people mentioned agree on the same story or remember things the way I remember them. Nor that they view things the way I do or feel the same I felt at the time.

This story is from my point of view, my perspective and how I remember things, how I felt about what happened. There are no right or wrong, good, or bad when it comes to our memories. It's just memories, events and decisions that had different consequences. I wrote this story to share how, despite years of trauma, dysfunction and hurt, one is still able to create a good life and make better choices. One can still find comfort and support within oneself, step outside the comfort-zone and create a more stable base for the next generation.

There was a time where I wore the "victim-label". I had a victim-mentality where everything just seemingly happened to me, for no reason, just like the society had taught. That; if someone offends you in any way, you're a victim and there's absolutely nothing you can do about it. It's not your fault, it's not your responsibility and it's not your issue in any shape or form, therefor you can't do anything about it, and you can't change anything. However, throughout the years I've learnt that I'm a co-creator to everything that happens in my adult life.

As a child, I was a victim. I had no power or influence to change my upbring. There were no room for me to change or do something about my life. The adults in my life had the responsibility and the duty to help me but they failed in their parental mission to do so. As an adult, however, I do have power and influence. There is room for me to make changes and to do something about whatever feels wrong or feels change worthy in my life. I have full responsibility for everything and everyone I allow into my life, how my life is and how it unfolds. All relationships I have had, all experiences, all situations and circumstances are something I co-created through both conscious and unconscious choices. These choices were based on what I had learned so far in my life and my then-knowledge about the world, the society, and people.

Before we go deeper into my story, I would like to inform you dear reader, that from very young age I've had a strong and close relationship to nature and the All, that I've chose to call the Creator. This Creator is, according to me, both female and male, and differ a lot from the "traditional" view of the Creator. My own spiritual belief was a very important component in my childhood, and is still today, very important to me. My relationship with the Creator is between me and the Creator, as well as my thoughts and ideas regarding spiritual and extradimensional thoughts. You as a reader have no obligations to have a certain spiritual or religious belief nor any thoughts or conceptions of spirituality, religion, or extradimensional understanding to read this book. I do ask however, that you do not mock, hate, or make fun of my personal conceptions of these beliefs, but accept and respect that this is how I see the world. It might not be in alignment with your personal beliefs, and that is okay. It doesn't have to be. You can be a conservative Christian, a Hindu, a Muslim, or a Satanist and still read this book from your own point of view and spiritual beliefs.

My thought regarding this book, like many other people's stories, is that someone might find comfort and support by my experiences and words. So, let's start, shall we?

CHAPTER ONE

Notes from therapy:

I'm about seven years old and sitting on the kitchen floor with my then five-year-old baby brother Arnie. We are building with wooden bricks. We are sitting in a corner, right next to the door to Arnie's room and he is constantly destroying what I'm building. He throws the bricks around as I'm building with them, and I get annoyed. I tell him to stop several times, but he just keeps going. Finally, I just hit him on the arm.

At that exact moment when I hit my brother, our father comes into the kitchen from the hall and sees me hit Arnie. He quickly walks up to us and shouts at me that I'm not allowed to hit my brother. He stands leaning over me and shouts in my face. I'm very scared, but I don't dare to show it. When I don't answer back, my father starts kicking me instead. He kicks me three or four times in the waist and then stomps on my legs.

It really hurts a lot, but I just stare at him and refuse to say anything or to show how much it really hurts or how sad I am inside.

Our mother sits in the living room next to the kitchen and watches TV. I want her to come and help me, but she doesn't. She never does. I feel very abandoned and unwanted. Our father stomps at me a few more times and says, "now you might have learned the lesson to not to hit your brother!" and just walks away. I stay quiet and just focus my gaze straight ahead. Arnie is quiet too. When our father has left the kitchen, Arnie starts playing again. I just want to get out of there, but I can't, my legs and my waist hurts too much. I struggle to hold back the tears and pinch myself hard in the hands to avoid thinking or feeling anything.

The next day at school, I have hard time walking and paying attention in class, because it hurts so much. The school nurse calls me in and talks to me. She asks about the pain and the bruising on my leg. I lie, saying that I fell with the bike the day before. She seems hesitant, so I add that she can talk to my sister who is in two grades above me and that she could also ask my best friend Emma, who is in the same class as me. The school nurse seems to be content with my explanation

Just reading the above memory, as well as the upcoming ones, could make one jump to the conclusion that my parents are evil or so-called monsters. But they are not evil, nor are they monsters. Terrible role-models- yes. But not evil. However, they were and are extremely hurt people. Hurt by family, hurt by society. And we as children were born in all that pain. And this is one of several examples of how living in a household filled with pain and hurt looked like.

Our home was emotionally cold, violent at times, lonely - always. I was born as the second child in a sibling group of a total of seven children. From what I have been told, I was never comforted as an infant, except by my father when he realized that I had probably been crying for a very long time. Maybe that's why I would rather prefer him than my mother during my childhood and my whole life, really. My mother believed children should "air their lungs" and not be "rewarded" by being lifted if crying, no matter how small the child was, so she simply ignored me until I fell silent. I've seen her do the same with my younger siblings, which increases the likelihood that she did the same with me. Her way of treating us children was never loving or caring, but empty, distant, and dismissive. She never gave one comfort, support, or help.

As a small child, I was angry and frustrated about this and many other things. I didn't understand what I had done wrong to be so rejected by her all the time. During my early adult years, I was very angry at her specifically, which is inevitable when growing up with emotional neglect, especially if it is an adult of the same sex as oneself who rejects one. If you have struggled to be seen and confirmed in your existence, and have only been dismissed, you will be angry at that person. I wasn't aware of the dynamics back then, I just walked around and was offended and angry at her, at my grandmother and at my big sister Jasmine, all female role models who could only teach me anger, hatred, rejection, and abuse.

Now as an adult, I realize that my mother was and is like a child herself, with a child's reasoning, a child's attitude and a child's self-preoccupation and attention seeking. She always competed for attention and does so to some extent even today. She has not been an adult parent to me or my siblings, but a small, lost girl in an adult woman's body. During all these years, she has acted based on the small child she was the first time she felt abandoned, alone and as an outsider.

To understand my parents' behaviors better, I needed to do a deep dive into the immediate family because I do not think that behaviors only appear in an individual. Most people are not born evil or wakes up one day and thinks that they should neglect and abuse their children. My thought is that there are underlying behaviors that are hereditary in a way. The behavior has emerged through an event or situation at one point, and as long as that event or maybe several events, are not noticed and treated, they will remain in the family and affect future generations. These behaviors can be seen as lingering diseases that are inscribed in one's DNA. Just as you have a predisposition for some physical issues, I believe that you can have a predisposition for dysfunctional relationships, behavioral problems, lack of connection and poor decision-making.

MY MOTHER

Expressing my feelings has always been a challenge for me, especially when it comes to describing my relationship with my parents and siblings. I am autistic, which has made the whole issue of attachment and the sense of community extra complicated for me.

As for my mother, I have never felt any real connection to her. Even though she was called 'Mom', there was never any genuine fellowship between us. To me, she was just an adult that I had to obey because of her age and role, not for any emotional closeness or understanding. My mother was physically present, but emotionally absent. It created a gap between us that has never been bridged. As a child, I tried to get her approval, or a kind word, but it never came. Instead, I learned that my feelings and needs didn't matter, and that my way of being was wrong. Every time I tried to approach her, I was met with what I then interpreted as coldness and rejection, which has left deep wounds in my heart.

Today I interpret her rejections more as anxiety, as if she is afraid of me. Afraid of how I function and how she will face this. It may sound strange, but that's the feeling I get; that she can't understand me, can't read me, can't "control" me and then it's better to just ignore it all and sacrifice the relationship, than to risk "failing" and maybe she's afraid of what it might mean for her? She has lived a very lonely and vulnerable life herself. Do you then, as the child in the adult body she is, want to expose yourself to more risks? My mother was and still is, like a stranger in my life, a shadow that was there but was never present. I think today that maybe living in a violent and threatening existence, makes someone becoming more of a shadow to protect oneself?

A mother's role in the family is to be a female role model for the children. This female role model should guide the children, especially any daughters, in how to behave as a woman. By this I mean how to set healthy boundaries, how to show yourself and others respect and how to use the female energy and knowledge in the family and in the world, in a good way. The mother I and my siblings had taught us to create dysfunctionality, emotional numbness and disrespect for oneself and others. We learned that our feelings and experiences were worth nothing. Our bodies were not our own, but everyone else's property to criticize and judge arbitrarily. Others had the right to denounce whether you were "thin and good looking" or "fat and ugly", whether you were "nice and kind" or "ugly and stupid". This is something my mother learned from her mother, who learned from her mother.

It's painful to realize, but the truth is that my relationship with my mother, as well as my father, has shaped my entire life. It has affected how I relate to other people and how I see myself. I've had to struggle to build a kind of self-esteem that isn't based on rejection, criticism, indifference, or mocking comments. Even if you are autistic, it doesn't mean that it doesn't hurt to be rejected or mocked for who you are.

Even today, the few times I run into her, I still feel a deep anxiety, but also a kind of sadness. She is still the same - distant, emotionally unavailable, and unable to give the love and warmth that a mother should give. Before, the grief was about the fact that I was still the child who longs for the mother I never had, today the grief is about the fact that she, as a human being, never felt welcome or loved either. I think it must hurt terribly within her, to live with that notion. She has mentioned it several times throughout my entire life, that she does not feel loved or welcome. And no, she is not loved by me, she is not welcome in my home. But she can't demand of me, or of my siblings, to be loved. Many of us carries too many wounds to be able to feel such feelings for her.

The family on my mother's maternal line goes back a long way. There are many well-read and knowledgeable people in the family tree as priests, merchants, and artists. Many families who were also most likely in cultural conflicts with each other, such as the Sami in the family who were assimilated into Swedish society, who eventually married the priests whose job it was to convert the Sami to Christian Swedes. Many seem to have moved around between Sápmi, Norway and Iceland and seem to have been rootless and restless. Which also reflected my grandmother very much, I think.

My biological grandfather was also a very restless and rootless soul, he mostly traveled around different countries and never settled down anywhere. His wandering life meant that he couldn't be there when my mother grew up. Honestly, I do not think he wanted to be a present father either, he was not known to be particularly caring. From what I've heard, he was abusive, threatening, overbearing and arrogant jerk. My own opinion is that he was absent, I only met him three times in my life before he passed away from cancer. I was about twelve years old at the time and I knew no more about him than what he did for a living and his reputation as an arrogant, egocentric womanizer who scattered children around him which he then, without much worry, just abandoned for the next woman or adventure. I do not really know what happened to him in his life, but whatever it is, it can't have been good.

My grandmother rarely mentioned him, and my mother talked only about her longing for him before he died. During her childhood, my mother had no friends and was severely bullied at school. That must have been a very, very painful upbringing. I do not know how much of her behavior is a result of absent parents, bullying and loneliness or how much is neurological or psychological. It is very difficult to put a finger on exactly what is going on inside her. She has always had a kind of aura of something…. odd. I think that is what others have felt as well, and maybe she also feels this oddity, but cannot describe very well? I don't know.

Of course, there is nothing wrong with being odd or strange. But as the animal we humans are, people usually senses if someone is wired very differently than most others. And when people are perceiving others as too different, they are distancing themselves or punishing this person, through bullying for example. It's a very primitive way of reacting to something we feel is strange or odd, but we are primates after all….

I am a different and odd person too and I am very different from my other siblings both in behavior and appearance and personality. I know what it is like to experience oneself as different and to notice that others perceive one as different and the exclusion that follows. But my mother… I didn't want to be alone with her at all. Being with her created a severe anxiety and insecurity. She wasn't someone I wanted to approach, and I'm wondering if other people feel that way too around her. If so, that's very sad. I think she wants to be kind and be perceived as a kind person. But I've always have had a hard time finding her inner goodness, even though I feel it's in there somewhere. Unfortunately, it's very, very difficult to notice.

During my childhood, before I understood how behaviors are inherited, developed, and recreated, I still tried to understand my mother's reasoning when she meted out punishments or when she made her decisions, but they were so extreme in their manifestations that it was never possible to predict what would happen next or what was expected to be done. One moment you could be locked in your room because you contradicted something, another time you could be you could be accused for "creating suicidal thoughts in her mind" and another time she could coldly claim she wished you were dead, because you were perceived as rowdy and messy.

There was never any logic or reason in my mother's actions, and it was scary to never know from one second to the next what punishment you would receive or when you would be subjected to something. One punishment I remember very well was one winter when I was nine years old. My mother felt that I had been mean to my brother Arnie because I did not let him play with my toys. For me, as an autistic person, it was unthinkable to let anyone else touch my things or be in my room. I hated the idea of having to deal with other people in my extremely private space. My toys weren't just toys for me; They were carefully organized and meant a lot. The dinosaur collection stood on a shelf of its own, classified by species and time. The dolls, which I hated but still got from my mother, grandmother, and aunts because they thought I should be like a "real" girl, were on another shelf. Usually completely untouched and in their packaging.

When our mother gave Arnie permission to help himself to *my* things in *my* room, I was extremely upset, stressed, and angry. I pushed him out of the room and slammed the door shut. I may well have said something unpleasant at the same time. But our mother didn't think I had the right to keep my room safe and couldn't understand why I became hysterical about the change and stress it meant for me. Instead, she thought it was reasonable to force me out into the winter darkness, late evening, and let me, with an iron skewer, hack holes in the frozen ground around the garden to put up fence posts.

My punishment was to create these post holes for her, in the middle of winter and without the right equipment. I was locked out and Jasmine had to keep watch through the windows in the living room to make sure I was doing the task. Arnie was given free rein in my room in the meantime, and I hacked the damn holes with all the hatred I could muster for my mother, Arnie and Jasmine. I hated them dearly then and on many other occasions. I don't know how or when she learned to act like that, but today I understand that she has been or is, mentally ill and that she probably has some kind of inherited mental disorder that affects empathy and the ability to reason. My mother was never the adult, loving role model I needed; Instead, she created an environment of dysfunctionality, emotional muteness, and disrespect. I have struggled to build up a self-esteem and understanding that my feelings and experiences are worth something, even though I never got it from her.

With the information I have today, it leans strongly towards that she probably has a borderline disorder. Of course, I can't make a diagnosis of her, any more than a diagnosis would explain everything about a person. However, her bizarre, extremely unstable, and impulsive behavior is consistent with how a person with borderline disorder might function. She could go from one extreme to the other in just a few seconds, and it was impossible to predict what reaction you would get. To her, everything was black or white, you were either good or evil, good, or bad, and you couldn't reason with her.

There are radical extremes in every direction and high unpredictability. I keep that information in the back of my head, simply to understand her better, and work on forgiving her for all the pain she caused and still causes. I don't say this to criticize her, but because she has never shown any empathy or sympathy for others. If you talk to her about your feelings, whether it's about someone dying or if you've got a serious illness, she quickly diverts the conversation to her own life. It's as if one's own experiences and feelings were never addressed. No matter how serious or emotional the topic is, the conversation always turns into a monologue about her problems, her sorrows, and her worries. You can mention something deeply personal and painful, but instead of being met with understanding or empathy, she begins to talk about her own experiences, often without any connection to what you have just shared.

This inability to listen and show empathy makes you feel even more isolated and invisible. It doesn't matter what you're talking about: her reactions are always self-centered. For example, if you try to talk about the grief of losing a loved one, she changes the subject to how difficult her own relationships have been or ar, or if you share the news of a serious diagnosis, she starts talking about her own health problems, no matter how trivial they may seem in comparison.

This dynamic makes it impossible to get the support and comfort you seek, and instead you are left with the feeling that your own worries are not worth paying attention to. Her lack of empathy and understanding creates a wall between us, unfortunately.

When I learned that my father had passed away, she called me – on that same day, just hours after I got the news- just to talk about how hurt she had been all those years in their relationship. I hadn't talked to her for some years at that point and I had to remind her that it was very hurtful and inappropriate of her to call me- their daughter, and cry in my ears about my father's former behavior, especially on the very same day I learned he had died.

It didn't occur to her that it was wrong. If you point out to her that she always diverts the conversation to be about herself, she usually starts crying, which makes it difficult to continue the conversation. Her tears come with accusations of how mean and stupid one is who never lets her talk about her experiences. She may say things like that no one ever cares about her or that she is always feel abandoned. These emotional outbursts can be so intense that they completely change the dynamics of the conversation, leaving you feeling guilty and ashamed for trying to express your own needs.

In extreme cases, she has said that it might be better if she took her own life. This is particularly hard to hear and creates an immediate and strong sense of responsibility and concern for her well-being. She uses these threats to manipulate and control, making one shy away from ever questioning her or trying to make one owns feelings heard. My mother's way of dealing with us children most often involved a form of emotional blackmail that was both harmful and destructive. When we talk about the absurd and rigid rules she imposed and the punishments she meted out, she refuses to acknowledge them. According to her, these events never happened, or as my grandmother put it, "You children can't have remembered it, you were children," as if our memory doesn't exist until we grow up.

This inability to accept and deal with criticism, combined with her extreme reactions, makes it impossible to have open communication. It's like walking on eggshells; Any attempt to talk about difficult topics can trigger a storm of emotions that you are not equipped to handle. This has created a deep sense of frustration and helplessness in me, and it took me over thirty years to gather the courage to speak up and set boundaries for how I accept being treated. It was a long and painful process to accept that she will never stand for what has been done from her side.

Today I understand that she probably has a personality disorder, which explains why she behaves the way she does. She can't really help her behavior, and therefore I can't expect her to change, either when it comes to this part or any other aspect of her behavior. It's simply not in her nature, and it's something I must simply accept. As a child, however, it was something completely different from okay. There were many times when I was so angry and disappointed in her because I couldn't understand how she worked. I didn't know why she couldn't show love or compassion, or why her reactions were always so extreme and unpredictable.

The anger and frustration I felt as a child was intense. It was difficult to handle and even harder to understand. I often felt powerless and alone, and those feelings stayed with me well into adulthood. It has taken time and a lot of reflection to come to the realization that her behavior was not intentionally cruel, but rather a result of her own mental health issues. With that realization, I have been able to begin to let go of some of the anger and disappointment I have been carrying. I have realized that I cannot change her and that it is not my responsibility to do so. Instead, I've learned to set boundaries and to protect myself from the damage her behavior can cause.

It was a difficult journey to reach this understanding, but it has also given me a deeper insight into how complex and multifaceted people can be. Even if I can't change her, I can change how I react to and deal with her behavior. And it has given me a sense of control and self-respect that I previously lacked.

MY GRANDMOTHER

Another complicated and dysfunctional figure in my life is my grandmother. As an infant, she was adopted and grew up in a home that, although safe, lacked emotions and was several miles away from the area of southern Sápmi where she was born. My memories of my grandmother's adoptive parents are stern, emotionally absent, and very, very old people. As a child, I had never seen anyone as old as them and I was afraid of their old age and frailty. They weren't threatening as people, but they were very boring and incredibly strict. I can imagine that the home did not invite much love, even though it offered routines, structure, and security. The few times my siblings and I visited them, I remember it being cold, stiff, and joyless, as if these people just existed without really living.

As children, we were expected to be quiet if we weren't spoken to, we weren't allowed to disturb with play or anything else. We were to sit still in certain places in the living room, with our backs straight and our hands in our laps. Children were not allowed to sit on the sofa, only at the large dining table and listen to the large wall clock that ticked slowly. Every minute felt like a funeral. We were not allowed to touch anything and certainly not run around. We were woken up at six o'clock and got 'morning porridge' at seven, punctually. Being five minutes late to the dinner table meant that no breakfast would be served, no matter the excuse.

The only thing I know about my grandmother's biological mother is that she was a lost soul with illegitimate children and complicated relationships before she married my grandmother's biological father and had a few more children. At that time, my grandmother had already been adopted to her new family. Being adopted and then being told that you have siblings who have been allowed to stay in the biological family can probably affect your psyche. I think this may have affected my grandmother's ability to be empathetic and sympathetic to others, including my mother.

Another thought that pops into my head occasionally, is that my grandmother most likely didn't want to have children at all but had it because it was expected of her as a woman. She is, in a way, an involuntary mother and grandmother who is just doing her duty. You can say what you want about her way of treating her own children and us grandchildren, but she was more supportive than expected during the upbringing that my siblings and I had.

There were many times during our childhood that we ended up with our grandmother, either because our parents actively chose for us to be there or because Child Protective Service's temporarily placed us with her. Although she always received us, it was clear that she didn't look forward to our visits. She was and is far from the typical image of a grandmother, someone who bake cookies, cuddles, or who listened with interest to what we had to say. She was and is the opposite. I have never baked any cookies with her and never hugged her. Instead of offering a warm embrace and caring words those times we ended up on her doorstep, we were met by a woman whose days were marked by severity and distance.

It was obvious that she only considered it her duty to receive us, but the emotional closeness or concern that many associate with a grandmother was rare. When we needed comfort or support in a difficult situation, for example with a beaten mother in the hospital and a father in local custody, we just had to settle for a "yeah, yeah." She was a symbol of stability and order but lacked the softness and love that children usually associate with their grandmothers. When we came to her, we were often met with a deep sigh and then we were told how badly behaved and poorly dressed we were. She has a conviction that it was good for children to be told how ugly, fat, horrible, bad, ill-mannered, or badly dressed they are. According to her, such comments would turn said children into obedient, well-dressed, and polite children in some way, and we were not allowed to contradict her. Sometimes she would just leave us where we stood, no matter where we were, if we, as grandchildren, spoke up and said that we at least had enough decency and sense not to say mean things to others the way she did. At such times, she just said that such horrible children as we did not deserve her presence, turned around and walked away from us. She absolutely could not accept being told off and was very easily offended in her self-invented authority. She didn't hesitate to try to suffocate us with shame and guilt if we spoke up. It took me over thirty years before I dared to speak up for real and tell her that I no longer bought her guilt tactics. I explained that she had to accept that her words and behavior hurt others and that we have the right to speak up. So no, my grandmother is not full of love or even compassion. However, she is full of duty. No one can take that away from her. She has been there, in her own way, no matter what. She was there. She didn't like it, she often didn't like us, but she opened her home to us, anyway. And that's always something.

Her true passion is to travel and meet people. That's when she blossoms, but she is strangely distanced and reserved even then. But there is a clear shift within her when she is allowed to travel around the world or talk about all her travels. Without children and grandchildren. I have a highly sporadic contact with her today, usually we just send each other a text message. I have no eager or desire to spend time with her, but I am still grateful that she has taken care of us after all. She could have said no, she could have given us all up to the foster care system, but she didn't. This hard-working single mother who was both emotionally and physically absent since she worked abroad a lot, was the mother my mother had.

MY FATHER

Well, if we go over to my father, he was a working alcoholic who worked in industry from six in the morning to five in the afternoon. When he got home, he was tired, irritated, and usually went to rest for a while on the couch. Then he went out to his garage and drank while repairing cars, which was an interest he had. He liked cars and he liked to tinker and fix things. He was clever in that way, extremely intelligent and probably actually a very sensitive person. Maybe that's why he became so incredibly aggressive when he drank?

With his background as an orphanage child and an unwelcome and abused foster child, he probably felt terribly abandoned, unloved and deeply alone. The pain and loneliness he carried was something I could feel strongly when I was a child. It was as if he had a bottomless despair inside him, tearing him apart from the inside, and I just wanted him to understand that he was indeed loved and that he was not alone. I was often very sad for him because he was always so angry and sad, I was sadder about his sadness, than how he treated me and my siblings or our mother.

His aggression and anger when he was drunk were difficult to deal with and created a constant atmosphere of fear and insecurity in our home. But I could see beyond the anger and irritation he showed outwardly, and instead see a man who was deeply hurt and alone. I remember how I often tried to reach out to him, show him love and understanding, but it was as if his pain was an impenetrable wall that prevented him from receiving any of what I was trying to give.

Despite his destructive behavior and alcohol abuse, I saw glimpses of his intelligence and ingenuity as he worked on the cars. It was as if in those moments he found a temporary refuge from his inner pain, and I couldn't help but admire how skilled and creative he was. His ability to fix things was one of the few ways he was able to express his talent and capacity, and it was tragic to see how his emotional wounds and alcohol addiction limited his potential.

To see him tormented by his demons and at the same time feel my own powerlessness was heartbreaking. I wanted so badly for him to find peace and understand how much he meant to me and my siblings. But I also realized that his pain was deep-rooted and that as a child, I didn't have the power to heal the wounds that his life had created

Despite that my mother also felt and feels very sad, abandoned, unloved and alone, which she has expressed herself, I have never had the same feelings for her as for my father, and I think it's because of the connection. Through therapy I have learned that there is an underlying attachment disorder between me and both my parents, but that the disorder is more severe between me and my mother than between me and my father. That's why my father's emotional storms touched me more than my mother's, and I did more for my father than for my mother.

One can consider it to be deeply unfair, and in a way it is. But it's also important to understand that I never felt any closeness or connection to my mother. I felt a certain connection to my father; He and I were and are quite similar in our personality, we are highly sensitive, like nature and tinkering with things. Much of my appearance also comes from him and honestly, I don't think my mother liked that. Although my father was usually angry and drunk, I could see his innermost being, the goodness that was deep within him. I wanted to bring it out, because I felt that he held so much love beyond all the pain he unfortunately focused on. This realization created a stronger connection between us, despite his flaws and destructive behavior. He could be a broken man, but he was also a man with the potential for great love and goodness, something I always felt and tried to achieve. With my mother, it was different. She was so emotionally absent in a way that made it impossible for me to feel any kind of connection. Even though she might also be filled with pain and loneliness, I had a hard time reaching her and felt no desire to do so.

The fact that I felt a certain attachment to my father, despite his alcoholism and aggression, says a lot about how complex and deep emotional bonds can be. The little spark of commonality and understanding I felt for him was enough to create a bridge between us, a bridge that was completely missing between me and my mother. This imbalance in attachment affected my upbringing and my view of my parents. I often felt divided, filled with contradictory feelings of love and disgust, hope and despair. But over time, I've learned to accept these feelings and understand their origins. It has helped me process my childhood and create a better understanding of myself and my relationships.

As a child and a young adult, I put a lot of effort on trying to make my father happy, proud and above all, I didn't want him to feel alone. In my little world, I thought my physical presence and my encouragement would help him feel less alone on the inside.

Despite my persistent attempts to cheer up my father, I don't think he could ever really understand it. He could never believe it and could never take it to heart. His inner dialogue was so critical and so strong that all the love he received from us children could never dampen the pain of his childhood. He was absent in many ways – partly by physically staying away from his family as best he could, partly by the terrifying black hole that was his insides. Even though he was aggressive, emotionally absent and a person you could never question, he was the one I turned to the most of my parents. At least I could feel if he was sober or drunk and how angry he was at the given moment. It gave me a little sense of control and I thought there was a certain logic in his behavior.

For many, it is difficult to understand or accept that there may be any logic behind domestic violence. Violence is often seen as something inexplicable and brutal, a pure manifestation of anger or frustration with no deeper cause than control or jealousy. But for me, growing up in such an environment, there was a certain logic behind my father's behavior, even if it was destructive. He only hit when he was angry, and he got angry most when he was drunk. Understanding this pattern gave me a sense of predictability in an otherwise chaotic and frightening world. I realized early on that he got drunk because he had pain in his soul. His pain was deep and rooted in his childhood as an orphanage child and unwelcome, abused foster child. He felt terribly abandoned, unloved, and deeply alone. It was as if his inner demons required alcohol to be silenced, but instead they only exacerbated his torment and made him violent.

My mother, who could be very stressful, also contributed to his anger, unfortunately. Many people believe that the party who is beaten in a relationship is completely innocent and has no responsibility in the matter, but I don't see it that way. I don't see any innocent adults in destructive relationships, only co-creators.

My parents' relationship was filled with conflict and tension, and for him, alcohol became a way to numb the emotions he couldn't handle. For me, it was logical that he did what he did. There was a certain predictability in his anger—I knew that when he drank, he would get angry, and when he got angry, he would hit. This predictability became a survival strategy for me; It helped me navigate my life and try to avoid situations that could trigger his violence.

As a child, you don't question that kind of logic; It is seen as normal and quickly becomes part of everyday life, especially if you have grown up with it from the very beginning and have nothing else to compare with. Understanding his behavior in this way helped me to manage my fears and to find some kind of stability in an otherwise unstable environment. This realization, while painful, has also given me a deeper understanding of how trauma and pain can manifest in destructive behaviors. It has taught me that behind every violent outburst there was a person who suffered, and while that doesn't justify the violence, it helps me to see beyond the actions and understand the underlying causes. This perspective has been crucial for my own healing process and to be able to forgive, not only my father, but also myself for the feelings of guilt and shame I have been carrying.

As a very young child from daycare to high school, I had a friend, Paulina, and later another friend, Elin (who became my truest friend through life), at grade school and high school. Around them were some other friends, we were a little gang in the end. Anyway, Elin and Paulina were my closest friends, the main ones, that I often hung out with at their home. However, I didn't really reflect on the fact that their parents didn't seem to quarrel and fight all the time. I was only there for short moments, what did I know about their lives after I left? Nothing.

In my world, domestic violence was normal, it wasn't really anything to talk about with friends or anyone else for that matter. I had been told early on to never tell other adults, like the school nurse or doctors because they, with the help of Child Protective Services, had the power to destroy the family union. The one who spoke up, was at fault, and no child wants to be at fault for ruining the family. Other's my age, why would I talk to them about my homelife? It was none of their business and really nothing I thought I needed to talk about. And they didn't notice either, at least not in the beginning, most probably because I seldomly invited them home. So, I kept my family's behavior to myself.

CHAPTER TWO

Notes from therapy:

"It's summer and I'm about 10 years old and my big sister Jasmine is 12 years old. We have summer holiday, and we play in the barn and in the hayloft above the barn. It is warm and sunny outside, but cool and nice up in the hayloft. When we are up in the hayloft, we hear tiny squeaky sounds coming from behind a hay bale. Curious about what it could be, we climb over the hay to get to the hay bale from which the sounds come. We find five little newborn kittens. We are overjoyed and wonder if it is wild cats or any of our outdoor cats that have given birth to them. We also know that we are not allowed to keep any animals other than the ones we already have, so we decide to keep the kitten's secret.

Our secret is a secret for about four days. Our mother has noticed that we often run out to the barn and stop us at such an occasion in the hall. She demands to know what we do in the barn. She does not like us keeping secrets from her. I'm lying and saying we're just playing and doing nothing special. Jasmine, on the other hand, can't keep quiet but talks about the kittens. We get a real scolding where we get to know exactly how stupid and disobedient, we have been and how disappointed our mother is at us. Then she goes into the kitchen and comes back with a cardboard box and duct tape. Just then neither I nor Jasmine understood what our mother was going to do. She demands that we take her to the kittens.

I try to negotiate with her and say I want to take care of them, only until they are big enough to get new homes. She doesn't listen but takes definite steps towards the barn. She demands that we show the way, which I refuse to do, but Jasmine obediently shows where the kittens are. I follow closely. We stand by the stairs to the hayloft and our mother pushes us forward and up the stairs. We get up and my sister points to the hay bale where the kittens are. Our mother steps forward and presses the box into my hands and tells us to put the kittens in it. I get worried and ask why. She angrily replies; "Because I say so!".

I tell her that it is not good to move baby animals and she replies that we should have thought about that before we decided to hide the kittens from her. I get angry at her because I think her answers and reasoning are stupid. I question how she thinks, which makes her even angrier. So, she roars to us to put the kittens in the box at once otherwise…

I hold the box and Jasmine carefully puts the kittens in it. Then we carry them gently to our mother. It squeaks from the box, and I resist the impulse to pull the box back. Our mother immediately goes down from the hay loft with the drawer in one hand. We follow her. I'm worried about the kittens. Our mother walks towards the car, opens the driver's door and jumps in with the box. She starts the car, with the door open. Then she gets out of the car again and takes the box with the squeaking kittens with her. She goes to the back of the car. There she opens the lid a little and tapes the box to the exhaust pipe. I shout to her "what are you doing ?!", Jasmine holds her hands to her ears and closes her eyes tightly. She's crying.

When our mother has taped the box, she walks up to us and orders us to look. I ask her to let the kittens go, I try to get her to remove the box, but she just grins and says that "this is what happens when you don't follow the rules." Then she goes to the car, jumps into the driver's seat and presses the accelerator pedal- It squeaks from the box for a while longer and I feel bad. I want to cry; I want to tear the box from the exhaust pipe but still I just stand there and can't understand how she can do this to innocent kittens.

When she turns off the car and steps out, she looks at us as if she has won something. She takes the box from the exhaust pipe, shakes it and when she doesn't hear anything squeaking from the box, she just goes to the dustbin and throws it away. Then she enters the house as if nothing has happened. Jasmine cries but says nothing. I'm terribly angry and wish it was our mother who died there instead of the kittens."

No matter how many years that passes, I will never forget that day when my mother gassed the kittens. I'll never forget the squeaking, nor the kitten's soft fur and tiny little paws. This action, to gas the kittens and force us to witness, as a punishment, was just one aspect of how our homelife was like. It's one thing to be beaten by an adult, a totally other thing to being forced to witness animal cruelty. The powerlessness you feel as a child, when you are forced to such things, can make the most empathetic and sympathetic person to become an emotionally rigid and unsympathetic person as an adult. I became that. I put on a mask of not caring, not showing how much it hurt. How much I hurt. Because very early on you have learned that everything you say and do, can and will be used against you in your own personal family court.

One can ponder upon what makes a parent to kill animals before the eyes of their children. I know for a fact that my mother hates feeling she's being lied to, and she hates feeling like she's being cheated of something. She told me so herself just a few weeks ago, before writing this down. That, along with the sense of needing to control everybody at every time might be the reason. As mentioned before, I do believe she has some form of borderline personality disorder. Control, a fear of being left out and hyper aggressions are part of the disorder. At the time of this event, we were nine people living on that farm, whereas half of the household was in the nursing-age. Maybe our mother was mad from all her experienced and imaginary rejections, the guilt, shame and anger she might and most likely do, carry? Maybe she was so damaged from everything in her life, that she just had to hurt anybody, even her own children?

I don't know exactly what went on in her mind at that time, but through studying behaviorism at the local university, I feel I have some academical knowledge to understand what might have been going on. In that moment, and in other apparently deranged moments. Martha Beck is one of my favorite authors. She writes in her book "The Way of Integrity" that violence is about intentionally inflicting pain, hurt and suffering onto others. Being angry is not the same thing as being violent. For many years, when my mother gassed those kittens, and when she punished my siblings and me, I thought she was angry. That's what I interpret from her actions and expression: mother is angry at me or us. It's very easy to mix anger and violence. But, as mentioned, it's not the same thing.

After reading Martha Beck's book, I realized that my mother most likely felt offended in her role as a Parent, and she expressed that as anger. My sister and I had departed from her rules, and she most likely had the intention to revenge this offense by punishing us. The kittens were just tools, she didn't even consider their well-being. Revenge and punishment are silly and primitive ways to restore the balance that have been disrupted by someone's actions. It could be that someone is questioning the rules, argue against the person or in other ways disrupts the person's authority. In this case, my mother's authority as a Parent. Through her actions, both the one with the kittens, and other situations where she behaved seemingly crazy or unpredictable, she might just have tried to restore her authority the only way she knew how.

She most likely viewed the situation as me and my sister robbing her of her power and authority, by acting independently and speaking up, and it might have been seen as a very unfair thing to do. And as mentioned before, she really hates feeling tricked or robbed of things. Anything. Just like her own mother, she couldn't and still can't handle being challenged. She is thankfully less aggressive and volatile today, due to age, but also that she's in therapy herself. Unfortunately, she still has issues discussing how her actions in the past was harmful to everyone. With help of a psychologist, I've tried to talk to her about this, but I'm only met with confusion, and she doesn't seem to want to understand. Therefor I'm left to speculate and trying to understand it myself, without her participation in this.

Every time I've tried to talk to her about it, I've been met with confusion and incomprehension. At first, she categorically denied that these or similar events had ever taken place. It was as if the memories and pain they represented did not exist in her world. After I asked a few cautious follow-up questions, her answers have changed. Then she has admitted that, yes, these events may have happened, but she believes that they are a thing of the past and should not be addressed now. Her defense has often been that we children were incredibly difficult and quarrelsome, and she wondered if we didn't have any understanding of how difficult *her* life was. So therefore, I must speculate and investigate without her active participation in it. It's a pity, I think we both would benefit and learn from talking about this together, in a healthy, balanced environment, like in family therapy.

If it was today, I don't think she would go as far as to kill cats, but she still threatens to commit suicide if one doesn't feel sorry for her. Suicidal threats are one of her standard-patterns, so it doesn't affect me at all today. As a child, it was a battle with anxiety and shame for being put through those threats, and the half-hearted actions she (and my father) put into the threat. But today, I don't care. It sounds harsh and mean, but it's not like that. It's just that those threats are so worn out in my family, that it lost all sense of alarm and seriousness. Unfortunately, since suicide threats have been so heavily used in my family, I don't even get a sense of urge when other people use it. It's just a word among other words.

Anyway, after the incident with the kittens, I battled intense feelings of shame and blame. Why didn't I just yank the box out of her hands? Why couldn't I stand up for the kittens or why couldn't I stand up for myself or my siblings when we all got hurt and abused? Well, I never learned how to. I was never taught that I had rights. Or that I had rights and obligations to protect myself as well as others. And I was a child, and by that, limited mentally, emotionally, and physically. All those harsh words I've been told, all the painful punishments I had to take and all those times I was told I didn't matter, I wasn't lovable, I was stupid, silly, powerless and a Nothing. All those words integrated my brain and became a latch that stopped me from acting and taking my responsibility as a human. As Iyanla Vanzant says, in her beautiful way of playing with words: response-ability. My ability to respond, was distorted.

And that's a behavioral pattern that can be seen throughout generations back in my family. To become a powerless bystander. That was a huge part of my behavioral pattern, and it affected me very negatively in all those situations and in situations to come.

Something I've learned through life, and especially in therapy, is that I couldn't have acted differently at those given points in time, since I didn't know how to act differently. I can't change the time. I can't change what's been done. It all must become life-lessons to learn.

Teachable moments. Moments when I learned that sometimes you don't have the power nor the ability to act. However, those moments are not forever. There will always be a time when you can and should take power, act, and take control. At those moments, you need to be forgiving to yourself for what you did or didn't do and forgive those that hurt you. Forgiveness is a process, and it takes time. During that time, you will do the same mistakes or make new ones until the pattern is broken.

CHAPTER THREE

None of my parents had the ability to comfort, support or show tenderness. The only physical touch I got, or as I ever remember was given, was when I was punished. I was never given a hug, I never held hands and I never sat in anyone's lap, reading together or just being close and kind. As an autistic person, I'm not that very fond of physical contact, but that wasn't the reason to why I grew up like that. I was undiagnosed until my adulthood, and even if I'm not very fond of being touched, I didn't flip out as autistic people can do when being touched. I just tense up and freeze. My parents never hugged, kissed, or showed tenderness to any of us children, so it was a common thing, to never show affection.

The first hug I got from my parents was when I was an adult and had moved away from home. It was never any emotions or affection behind the hug, it was just "oh-hello-nice-to-see-you" kind of hug, and every hug after that. Emotionally distant hugs based the social code of mandatory hugging friends and family when seeing each other.

To me, it felt more like hugging a mannequin, that's how distant my parents appeared to be. They were there physically, but there was no contact on the inside. It hurt me that they were and are so empty, so distant and foreign. This inability to show affection and emotions before us children, taught us that we didn't deserve love and kindness. We learned that so called "love" is filled with pain, demands, terms and offenses. We learned that one must endure physical, emotional, and mental abuse to be accepted and to belong. The kind of "love" that was advocated in our home, was never love. It was a separation and a war for survival.

It is easy to think a lot of negative things regarding my parents' behavior, and much of what I have written down, isn't the kindest things to describe. But it's important to understand the context in which they were born and raised, as well as the context they created together for me and my siblings. Both parents had severe trauma from their own childhoods and they both passed that onto each other as well as us, their children. They were never evil people. They did hurtful and mean things yes, but they were never genuinely evil.

It's just that they had never learned how to show respect, love, affection, or emotions in a healthy way. Nobody had taught them about relationships, society, or parenting. All they had learned was to be absent, cold, distant, blame others, create conflicts, and provoke. And that's what they did.

My parents had a very, very violent relationship with each other and to us as children. The violence was sometimes physical, with kicks, slaps, or pushes, but mostly it was emotional, mental, and verbal abuse that took place. Almost every day was filled with expletives, mocking and verbal offenses. Sometimes we were forced to watch when the physically abused each other and were then asked to "pick sides", or we were asked to tell who was right and who was wrong. Sometimes we had to watch as a sibling was being tormented and abused as some sort of "lesson" to not make the same "mistake" as the abused sibling did. This simply was their way of child upbring.

I know that in society today, it's often said that when domestic violence takes place, the one adult on the receiving end of the abuse, is a victim. This might make some people offended, but I can't see the receiving partner as a victim. It's provocative, I know, but I consider it to be wrong to put all the responsibility for the violence only on the aggressor. When the abuse and violence is an occurring pattern in a household, I consider all adults being equally responsible. The first slap is the physical culmination of other dysfunctional patterns. It's not always foreseeable. But the second and the third slaps, pushes, knock outs, then you are aware. And then you are making a choice to stay in that relationship. And according to me, one must own up to that choice, no matter how painful it is to admit.

But, if we're not forced into a relationship by societal and family structures, we all choose our relationships. No woman or man will ever get my sympathy for staying in an abusive relationship. I'll never see people leaving an abusive relationship as a "survivor" or a "victim", simply because they are not. They are adults, making painful decisions and choosing painful experiences.

Another provocative train of thought is that my mother provoked much of the abuse she endured, and we as children had to witness. Either it was by choice or through unconscious behaviors. She stayed in the relationship with an aggressor and she herself had concerning behavioral issues. She herself abused us verbally, mentally, and emotionally. She created much of her pain herself, just like each of us children came to do as adults. I'm very happy that now adays, children are considered victims of crime when it comes to domestic violence, and I hope that in long term, both parents and caregivers that creates domestic violence get charged for child abuse. It may sound mercilessly, but it is a fact that anyone who fails – consciously or unconsciously- to protect children from violence, are as guilty for neglect and abuse, as the aggressor. The adults in such relationship clearly doesn't prioritize the welfare and the safety of the children and shouldn't be allowed custody if the violence is present.

A parent's job is to protect the children and prioritize their well-being and make sure they grow up to become functional and balanced citizens in society. Parents and caregivers that are stuck in domestic violence, are not doing any of that. My parents didn't prioritize to create a sense of belonging or community within the family. Each of us children, all seven of us, were raised in dysfunction and separation, just like all the children growing up in abusive homes.

No one of us got the chance to love each other unconditionally and not to love each other as a family. We were never siblings, and they were never parents, these are just concepts that I use in this book to make it more readable. We were and still are more like strangers that just happens to share genetic material and a household with two adult individuals that fought for power and space in the household. And we as children had the same behavior: we fought for power, for space and acceptance. This kind of upbring created deep and long-lasting scars within us all. No one of us has to this day, managed to create healthy, intimate relationships with other people. We get in and out of destructive relationships with others and with ourselves.

My self-destruction started very early. At age of six I already had an eating disorder. I actively restricted my diet, did excessive workouts, checked my BMI several times a day and used workout as a punishment if I had "sinned" by eating more than I had decided for. Even if it was a teaspoon more tea or one bite too much on the only sandwich, I allowed myself to eat for breakfast, then I had to punish myself by doing fifty sit-ups before I could go to school (which I biked or walked to, it was about four kilometers). My eating disorder was undiscovered for over ten years, since the norm and culture around that time was to be very slim, thin, and fit. I was praised for my thinness, by my mother and my grandmother, my mother's friends and other adults that openly praised and envied my thinness. And if diets were the way to at least some amount of acknowledgement and approval by my family, then dieting I did.

I also battled with severe anxiety, suicidal thoughts, and self-harm. My first suicide attempt took place when I was ten years old. I tried to freeze to death but didn't have the patience to lay there and die in a pile of snow. I had dressed down to a tee and shorts, taken a cold shower with the clothes on and went outside to die. But it was boring, so I went inside again and pretended it never happened. My parents never noticed anything, and I never told anyone. But on the inside, there was this big hole filled with self-hate and feelings of being unwanted, unloved and a human failure.

I never felt I belong anywhere, always felt and still feel like an imposter, which affects me even to this day. It's very hard to feel a connection to my heritage, it doesn't feel like I have the "right" to call myself a Sámi or a Swedish-Finnish person, or anything else for that matter. It doesn't feel like I have the competence to be anybody, at all, and that feeling makes it hard to put oneself out there, in society, in the world. It makes one keep restraining oneself as much as possible just to avoid being "found out". That others might "find out" that you don't belong there, that you don't count, and you're not accepted by any means.

At my current job, many people think that I know exactly what I'm doing, but they don't know the daily fight I have with those demons of worthlessness and imposter-syndrome. As an autistic person, I have learned to mask my functioning and pretend to be normal, which increases the feeling of being fake. This masking is an ongoing spectacle where I try to adapt to norms and expectations that do not suit me or my way of functioning at all.

It's exhausting to pretend to like social contexts, to pretend that it doesn't physically hurt my mind and body with all the impressions that just press on and chafe against me. It is exhausting to "cold talk" or be interrupted in what you are doing or to keep track of just about everything that needs to be done. This makes me often feel like a fraud, someone who doesn't belong or is good enough, someone who can't expose how things really are, because the lesson is; No one cares, it's me who is wrong.

My first year of work was a constant struggle. Every day I was convinced that I would be fired, that I would be exposed as incompetent. Despite having a bachelor's degree and the right knowledge in the right field for the job, I still felt and feels like a fraud. Despite being overqualified for my job, I still stay stuck in this underpaid and dead-end position, just because I don't feel worthy to do anything else. This is a direct result of growing up with values that pushes one down, making the child small and insignificant. This is often the outcome of a dysfunctional childhood, of growing up with a set of values that are based on oppressing, belittling and degrading others.

This feeling of inadequacy has put me in a work situation where I am not only underpaid, but also have a huge amount of stress and really hard to qualify further in any direction. It's like a vicious circle where my own insecurities and the constant masking prevent me from taking other steps in my professional life. I live with a constant fear of being exposed, that someone will see through my façade and realize that I don't really belong there.

Living with these feelings affects me deeply. I often feel like a stranger in my own life, someone who constantly must play a role in order to be accepted and understood. This is what leads many people from destructive homes to be "savvy" with low-pay and stressed out, seemingly stuck in jobs that lead nowhere. However, this is not an excuse not to put in more effort or not to grow as a person. Just because it looks a certain way and has been a certain way for a long time, doesn't mean it always has to be that way. You should never stop at the fact that this is how it has been, and this is how it will always be (and it comes from me who likes to hold on to the safe and predictable)!

I strongly believe that you owe it to yourself to do your best to go beyond your childhood, and your way of functioning. What I mean is that it is difficult to break a learned behavior, and even more difficult if you have a different way of functioning.

Self-criticism, negative thoughts, low self-esteem, and low self-esteem are learned thoughts and thoughts are behaviors. They are very difficult to identify and to rebuild. Add to that belonging to two minority groups that in Swedish society are viewed in a degrading way with racist prejudices and stereotypes glued to each group, and you have further learned notions that you need to get past.

I've come to learn that as an adult, you owe it to yourself and your children (if you have any), to outgrow your family beliefs and limits. It's hard, *really* hard, to change those behaviors you've been taught as a child. It's a hard pill to swallow, to understand and learn your own participation of the life you've created for yourself, based on lies and beliefs that have been told to you and about you, from your family and the society. However, thoughts are behaviors, and behaviors are changeable.

Add to that belonging to two minority groups that in Swedish society are viewed in a degrading way with racist prejudices and stereotypes glued to each group, and you have further learned notions that you need to get past.

All beliefs, both those that abusive parents teach you and those that society teaches you about being Sami or Swedish Finns, for example, are all based on the idea that you should stay in your place at the bottom of the hierarchy, not take care of yourself and understand that you are stupid, worthless and deserve whatever you encounter in the form of oppression and degrading words and actions. That as a being, one should not expect love, care or belonging.

Don't invoke human rights and don't think that you are somebody special. But know that others have rights you don't have, the right to tell you who you are and define you from their perspective, only because of your heritage. You're not allowed to be your own reference point, but you must relate to other people's ideas and references about you and therefor what and who you are.

Speaking of love and care, despite all the violence, my parents claimed that they loved each other, even though they almost never showed any affection for each other. I can only remember two times I've seen them kiss, then it was with an anxiety charge so strong that you backed back out of the room. The anxiety and stress literally oozed around both, and it was very unpleasant to take part in. By claiming that they loved each other and at the same time tried to kill each other and make life as chaotic as possible for us children, they taught us that love is something that involves violations and limitations of some kind. That love means that you are beaten, devalued, punished, and violated.

That form of "love" is what many people imagine to be "true love" and it is usually based on having learned that idea as a child. It is what you have seen and perceived during your childhood years, and it becomes the template you unconsciously search for. It is not the same as not being able to make other decisions, it is only an explanation, never an excuse. In short, there are no excuses for continuing a destructive relationship or lifestyle.

Another thing that many parents in abusive relationships like to claim, and my parents were no exception, is the claim that they were only together for the sake of us children. It is a statement that has disastrous consequences for the children who grow up with that view; that mom or dad gets hit, because of me. Such a statement taught us children that we were the reason, the very root cause, of the dysfunctional behaviors of others. By existing, we were the origin and thus responsible for the pain of others. It was our fault that it was the way it was in our family. If we children hadn't existed, they would never have lived together as long as they did and then they wouldn't have argued as much as they did.

I believed this wholeheartedly for many years, but during my teenage years I began to doubt it. Somewhere inside me the feeling gnawed that it wasn't entirely true that it was our fault or our responsibility that they argued and fought so much.

The idea that they would feel better living apart grew up, because the most logical thing would be that if they don't live together, they can't argue with each other in the same way. I didn't have any thoughts about alternating living, we children could take care of ourselves, we did that pretty much all the time anyway, so if they had abandoned us physically it wouldn't have made any difference.

Through this upbringing and this mindset that you stick together for the sake of the children, that you still love each other even though you hurt each other, I learned to allow bad treatment and lack of respect towards me as a person. I learned that even though someone hurts me physically or mentally, I should still show up for family, help them, and do what is expected in every given situation and every given relationship. I would be dutiful and submissive, and be at the mercy of others, even if it hurt mentally, psychologically, and physically.

My siblings still live by that, which I only understood a couple of months ago, when we met after a loss within the family, which I will tell you about later. In their world, it was obvious that you would show up, no matter how bullied and offended you get in the meantime. For them, love is to remain offended. Oliver said it himself: that love is to endure violations. If you love someone, you put up with it, then it's okay to be treated badly. For the one who treats someone badly, they have the right to offend, mock and humiliate because that is how you shows "love".

We disagree there. Over the years I have learned differently. In my new world, you can love someone and still say goodbye to that person while they are alive. You have no obligations to show up for people who treat you badly. Everyone has a duty to themselves, and especially a duty to any children, to ensure that one does not get hurt or mistreated. Sure, it's easy to say this, to "stand up for yourself, set boundaries!" It's very easy. In the mind.

Converting the thoughts into action, that is the difficult part. It is extremely difficult to resist the impulse to please others, the anxiety that follows shortly after you have said no, set a boundary, can remain for several hours afterwards, as well as all the thoughts "did I do the right thing now?" What happens now, will I be punished? What if that person hates me now?" When you have never been taught to sit with these feelings and thoughts or learn to speak up and expect to be respected, this period becomes terribly stressful, and anxiety ridden. It gets better with time, but as with anything else, it takes time to learn to function in a different way.

Sure, you can consider that it would be better if you had a different upbringing, then you would never have had to reprogram yourself in the same way, but I believe you get the upbringing you need in life. That you have the life you are supposed to have, no matter what it looks like, to learn something in this life. By learning things about one's upbring, and the people one grows up around, can help one become a better person for oneself and in before the Creator and thus do good in the world and the universe. You can choose to continue suffering and you can choose to use the suffering for something developing and inspiring. For a long time, I used my and my family's suffering to suffer some more.

Notes from therapy:

"It's spring or early summer, I'm not sure which. What I'm sure of is that I'm around six or seven years old and I'm wearing a red-white-checkered dress. I like that dress. It's hot outside and I'm walking barefoot across the lawn between the house and our dad's garage. My dad has been away for a short while, he does that sometimes when he's angry and sad. Then he goes to his garage and tinkers with cars.

I feel so sorry for him, that he is so sad and angry all the time. I want to be able to comfort him, show him that he is not at all as alone as he feels he is. As I walk towards the garage, I have a lump in my stomach that grows the closer I get to the garage door. My whole body is shaking with fear, and I don't really want to go in there because I'm afraid he'll yell at me or throw things at me. He can do that when he's really angry.

Ignoring my fear, I open the garage door anyway and hear his car running. It's a small car that our father uses for work. The garage door on the other side of the door is open and the sun is shining outside. I see a gray hose taped with silver tape to the exhaust pipe. The hose leads into the car through the window on the driver's side. The window is almost completely raised, and the hose is stuck between the window and the door frame. My dad sits in the car and just looks straight ahead. I walk barefoot across the concrete floor and at first just watch, because I don't really know what's going on, but I know it's probably nothing good.

I also don't dare knock on the window in case he yells at me or hits me. I am very tense and hug my hands for quite some time. Then I muster up the courage and open the car door. The car is full of exhaust fumes and my dad turns to me with a blank look in his eyes. I ask him to come in and get no answer. Then either I or he reaches for the steering wheel and turns the key. The car falls silent, and the exhaust gases slowly dissipate into the surrounding air. It smells strongly and stings the eyes and lungs. Coughing, I ask my dad one more time to come in and he gets out of the car and pulls off the hose which he just tosses to the side. He coughs occasionally and seems sluggish and slower than he usually is.

I lead him into the house but stop several times to make sure he follows. He doesn't say anything at all, only coughs occasionally. I keep a certain distance from him all the time, feeling scared and insecure. Once inside, he goes to the living room and watches TV without saying a word and without looking at me. I go into my room which I then share with Jasmine. I put in my favorite Michael Jackson "Thriller" cassette and start drawing. I don't tell anyone because I don't know that there is anything to tell. "

There have been times when both my parents have been so unhappy that they have tried to commit suicide. My father was the one who made the most active attempts, my mother made more half-hearted ones and threatened the most to commit suicide to get attention, without following up with actual actions. As children, Jasmine and I had to call the police several times to find our father who had disappeared in a fit of rage with the threat of never returning and that it would be our mother's and we children's fault to bear. This was so normalized in our family that I never got around to telling anyone else about it. No one had taught me that it was wrong or that our parents had really needed psychiatric help and medication.

But even though it was more normal than abnormal for our parents to threaten suicide or actively try to commit suicide, it created a void inside me that I didn't discover until I was an adult. A spot in my soul that gave rise to severe separation and death anxiety where I couldn't relax at all in case someone died. Almost every time my father disappeared and had mentioned that he was going to kill himself, it was up to me to call the police. Jasmine was usually too scared to make the call and our mother never cared. She would just shrug her shoulders with a "oh well" and walk away.

Notes from therapy:

"I see on the caller ID that it is my father calling from the cabin he lives in. I'm very happy that he's calling but he doesn't seem happy that I'm answering. But he also doesn't ask to talk to anyone else. He's slurring and rambling, so I understand he's drunk, which makes

me sad inside. He tells me that he will "fix everything" and I ask what he means.

He gets annoyed and tells me to just fuck off. So, I ask instead when he comes home again. He replies that since my mother is a "damn bitch" and he is just a "failure" he doesn't need to come home anymore. I then wonder if he will live in the cabin forever. He angrily replies no and that he will fix things it now and I must "give up looking for him". This worries me and I ask what he means. He blurts out that he is going to blast his skull off in his car and that he has left a note under a sewing machine in the cabin. He repeats once again that I should not look for him and hangs up."

My father often lived in his sister's summer cottage, beautifully situated by a lake, and surrounded by a forest. He has tried to die out there many times and I wonder if my aunt really knows about all the times her summer cottage has been turned into a police base in the search for my father. I don't think so.

On the aforementioned occasion, the police found my father in his car together with a shotgun that he had managed to get hold of. He was thoroughly drunk but did not resist, but willingly accompanied them to a drunken cell to sleep it off. I was the one who talked to the police in the search for him, despite my small age. At that time, mobile phones were very rare and terribly clumsy and unwieldy, so we only had one wall-mounted landline phone.

My opinion was and still is today, that my mother would actually think it would be a relief if he succeeded in his suicide attempts, then she wouldn't have to deal with the relationship. It would be an easy ticket out of the relationship and would also give her an even stronger victim status: the poor abused woman whose husband killed himself and left her alone with – then – three children. It may sound mean to write it out like that, but she was and still is today very much to be a victim of various circumstances.

It is part of her identity and behavioral profile and of course it can be frustrating at times, but I have to accept that this is how she chooses to have her life.

I no longer have to play along with her game. My belief is that she chooses this behavior time and time again because it somehow helps her cope with life. It helps her avoid responsibility for the relationships she has created over the years and the situations that are the consequences of those choices. It might help her bear the guilt and shame that she may be carrying, and it might help her bear the pain that she absolutely carries. Avoiding responsibility is a behavior that doesn't just appear out of thin air, it's a learned behavior. For my mother, no one was there to teach her to do things differently. She was never taught to stand up for herself or to break destructiveness. So, she simply couldn't do anything differently at the time.

I don't have to play along in her game anymore. She chooses this behavior time after time because it somehow helps her cope with life. It helps her avoid responsibility for the relationships she has created over the years and the situations that are the consequences of those choices. It might help her carry the guilt and shame that she might carry, and it might help her carry the pain that she absolutely carries. Avoiding responsibility is a behavior that doesn't just appear out of thin air, it's a learned behavior. For my mother, no one was there to teach her to do differently. She was never taught to stand up for herself or to break destructiveness. She simply couldn't do otherwise at the time.

Part of the healing from childhood trauma has been to simply understand and accept that neither my mother nor my father nor my siblings nor myself, could do otherwise. None of us knew better and it must be okay that this is the case. Another part of healing, for me, is to come to terms with what I have perceived as my mother's betrayal of me as her daughter, and that is a constant reconciliation, an ongoing process of constant transformation. That is why she is portrayed in a slightly different way in this story, precisely because she and I have never had a direct connection nor a joyful relationship.

I need to put a focus on what weighs me down and see her from other perspectives. She wasn't just that person that many people would label as "the mean mother", she was never even mean, just very disturbed, and unhappy. I want to understand, for myself, how she functioned and did what she did, and I would like others to understand that the people you have in your life who behave badly, do it for a reason. Nothing is black or white. There are reasons for their behaviors and it's not always obvious what those reasons are.

Unraveling my parents' and my own behaviors in this book is a way of taking responsibility for my own part and stand up for the situations I created as an adult. This avoiding taking responsibility was something that both my parents and I used to be professionals at and it's something I've noticed that many have a black belt in, today: not taking responsibility for one's life and their actions and consequences. It was always someone else's fault that my parents fought, drank, abused medication and that we had more reports and investigations at the social services than we - combined - had dentist visits in my first seventeen years of life. In the story I told myself, about myself, my parents' shortcomings and violent behavior were about me or about my siblings.

I knew that the adults did wrong, that they were hurt in some way, I knew that they behaved badly, but all this guilt that especially my mother, many times my father and sometimes even my grandmother put on us children, told me that we as children were complicit in what happened. That the fault was largely ours. This approach appears occasionally in my life, even today. If something happens at work, no matter what it is, I get anxious, examine myself if it's something I've done wrong. It's automatic and every time I have to tell myself that on most occasions, I don't even have anything to do with whatever is going on, and I'm free to go.

What I learned as a child was that I was a problem because I existed, because I was often aggressive as a child, because I spoke up, hit back at my siblings, etc., something that in psychologists' language is called being "dysregulated", in other words, out of balance.

My siblings and I were a problem because we too fought, screamed, argued, or hurt ourselves or each other. So, we made the parents angry, by unconsciously reacting to the upbringing we received, because we were all dysregulated. They believed that we children were to blame for the adults' behavior. None of our parents tolerated that you spoke up or resisted, then you were punished immediately. Either I have a slow learning curve, or I was just obstinate, but since I was the one who most often spoke up and spoke out, I was also the one who was punished the most, before my second youngest baby brother Oliver came into the world, then we had to share that place.

This is also related to my previously mentioned thoughts that my mother possibly has a borderline disorder. A parent with borderline disorder tends to treat their children differently in an extreme way. Some children are seen as "good" (the children who obey blindly) and others are seen as "evil" (the children who speak up and resist). There is no "in-between", no grayscale, it is black or white, you are a "good" child or a "bad" child, entirely based on what the adult thinks is good or bad.

You don't even have to have committed a serious offence, such as stealing money or a car, but simply that you are not what the adult has imagined you to be. Oliver and I were not what our mother imagined us to be. Both of us were and are extremely similar our father in appearance and we were more difficult to control than the others in the sibling group, even with threats or violence.

Although we were all mistreated in different ways, Oliver and I were met with more disgust and irritation than the others. As an example: it was only Arnie and our youngest brother Fredric who were allowed to use the shower at home. No one else was allowed to do so. We had both a shower and a jacuzzi, but we were not allowed to use them. We were only allowed to shower after PE-class at school or at the local bathhouse. The justification was that it would cost too much in water costs, which today feels like an absurdum since a monthly membership card at the bathhouse for at least five children must have cost money as well. Anyway, we weren't allowed to use the shower at home. We were also not allowed to use whatever towels we wanted, but the five of us had to share three bath towels and a bottle of shampoo. Jasmine and I were responsible for taking our siblings to the bathhouse every other day, so that we would not be at home, we were also the ones who were responsible for the safety of the younger children on site. At that time, we were between eleven and thirteen years old and our siblings around two and three years old. Oliver and I had to share a really worn towel because we were considered "dirty", according to others in the family. It was my responsibility to look after Oliver because Jasmine didn't want that responsibility.

Other examples: Oliver was unfortunately the one who was rejected the most and many siblings followed our mother's example in how we should be treated. Thus, bullying and ostracism were part of the siblings' attitudes and treatment of us, and above all of Oliver.

He was often sick and malnourished because we were allowed to eat every day, and if it was food, at least for Oliver, it had to be apple sauce with spittoons from Fredric or cornflakes with water. Our mother had put padlocks on the pantry, refrigerator, and freezer, because we were not allowed access to food. It was only Jasmine, Arnie and Fredric who were allowed to have access to the food.

The rest of us were not allowed to drink water unless we had asked for it first, and if we got a no, we were simply not allowed to drink water. We were also not allowed to go to the toilet without permission. Oliver was usually beaten up by Fredric. He often suffered from unhealed fractures, burns (a sibling tried to light him on fire for "fun") and infections, and rarely received any care for this.

During a routine check-up at the pediatrician, for example, it was discovered that Oliver had sepsis, as he was lethargic, pale, and very ill, where our mother tried to avert it all by saying "no, he's not that sick". He was hospitalized anyway and was in intensive care for three days. At that time, he had not even reached the age of four. Our mother believed that he had caused the sepsis himself to get attention. It was that level of morbidity and insanity.

I didn't get treated as bad as Oliver, but I was often scolded and punished because I tried my best to protect him from the violence he was suffering. It was usually said that I shouldn't interfere and that I shouldn't care. But I couldn't help but care. I wanted him to be well, even if it affected both of us in the form of additional punishments for me, such as locking up for a whole day, doing some heavy chore in the yard or not being allowed to go on a trip.

I know that not letting me go on holiday trips to Greece, Thailand and Bulgaria was meant as a punishment on my mother's part. But it was more of a vacation for me to be at home with my father. It was peace and quiet. No fights, no conflicts and above all; Not a lot of people, crowds, noise, and strange things. I never told her that I was looking forward to these "punishments", fearing that she would force me along just so I wouldn't enjoy my "punishment." Oliver got to go on these holiday trips sometimes, and sometimes he and Sandra got to stay with our grandmother instead while the others went away. I don't know how the two of them took this, but my hope is that they also had a nice and quiet time.

CHAPTER FIVE

Notes from therapy:

"It's winter, just after New Year's and I'm about 9.5 years old. My youngest siblings are a couple of months old. Our parents have been arguing and fighting all Christmas holiday. One day just before the start of school, two social workers and a couple of policemen suddenly come to our house. My father is at work, and I am at home with our mother and all siblings (five). I open the door when the party knocks and I want to know who they are, but they just ask me to go get my mother.

I don't have to go get her, because she comes hurrying through the kitchen towards the hall. I want to know if something has happened to my father but get no answer. I stand in the kitchen and try to hear what is being said in the hall when all the adults come in and take off their shoes and jackets. One policeman remains outside while the other policeman goes inside with the two female social workers who, to my mind, look old and serious.

My mother talks fast and stressed and takes no notice of me standing against a wall trying to listen to what they are saying. Unfortunately, I can't hear very well, the adults talk quickly and softly.

The group enters the kitchen and sits down at the dining table. Only then does my mother discover that I am still in the kitchen and tells me to go to my siblings who are in another room. She uses a tone she never uses otherwise; she is unusually kind and caring in her voice, which worries me. She only has that tone when social workers and police are around, and she doesn't want us to expose her or how we really are at home. I glare at her angrily but walk out of the kitchen and into my siblings, who are in our parents' bedroom on the other side of the living room. I know it's not worth saying anything then and there.

I really don't like the situation; it makes me scared and insecure. Jasmine is sitting with our younger siblings entertaining them when I come in. I tell her that social workers and the police are with us and are talking to our mother. She immediately becomes very worried and sad. She wonders what they want, and I ignore answering her, I don't know what they want either. Instead, I go and sit with the youngest and smallest brother, Oliver. Playing a little with him while keeping a close eye on the door into the room.

After what feels like an eternity, one of the social workers enters the room. She asks to talk to us big kids, I politely reply that it's fine, but I don't trust her for a second. The woman sits down on a nearby chair and clears her throat. In her hand she has a folder with a lot of papers in it.

She asks us how we are at home. Jasmine doesn't answer but looks away. I consider telling it like it is but know what the consequences are: our parents will end up in jail or kill themselves and we siblings will never see each other again and it will be my fault. So, I answer that it's okay at home.

She asks how we feel about our father, I answer that he is a good father and wonder why they never ask how *our mother is. I think it is unfair for them to only listen to our mother and never ask our father how he is doing.*

The social worker asks if our father drinks a lot, and Jasmine and I answer that it does happen...She further asks if our father beats our mother and I answer that they both fight and argue. Jasmine gives me a warning look not to say too much. The woman tells us that they (Child Protective Services and the police) have visited us several times because of violent arguing and alcohol. I just shrug. The woman looks around, at the messy room and at us children sitting on the floor. She excuses herself and leaves the room.

Jasmine slaps my arm and hisses at me that I should have kept quiet, that I might have ruined the whole family. I don't reply but focus on Oliver in my arms. Then our mother enters the room together with the other social worker. They say we should move. Now at once.

At first, I don't understand what she means, but thought she meant we should move off the floor, so I stand up with Oliver in my arms. Our mother is clearly stressed and tells us that we must hurry to pack the essentials and tears out children's clothes, diapers, and her own clothes from the closets in the room.

The social worker tells us matter-of-factly that we are going to move to a sheltered accommodation near the school that I, Jasmine and Arnie go to. I am very confused. Our father is at work, our parents hadn't argued today, why would we move right now? Our mother tells me and Jasmine to go to our rooms and pack clothes and bedding now at once. I hand Oliver over to the social worker and go to my room.

In the kitchen there is one policeman and the other social worker. They talk quietly to each other and give me and my sister a weird look as we pass the kitchen to get to our rooms. I need to pass Arnie's room to get to my room. Arnie is sitting on the floor playing with Lego. I tell him we're moving now, that he needs to pack. He gets up and runs out of the room. I roll my eyes and go into my room. I feel very empty inside, scared, and confused. I look at my things, my desk and wonder if I must leave everything forever.

Then I take my school bag and fill it with drawing paper, pencils, and books. I take out the few clothes I own and put them in a neat pile on the bed. I put my favorite cassette tapes and my tape player next to the clothes. Looking at my plants and hoping that someone- anyone- remembers to water them, because I love them dearly. They are my friends, my family. I say goodbye to each little plant and give them a kiss each, except my cacti, I pet them between the thorns. Telling them I have to be gone for a while, maybe forever.

I would love to take them all with me, but I have a feeling it won't work. Then I go out to the kitchen and get two plastic bags. The police and social workers remain in the kitchen, talking quietly, but they fall silent when they see me. I take the plastic bags and go back into my room and pack everything on the bed. Then I fold my duvet, my sheet and put my pillow on top. I hear my mother helping Arnie in the next room. I open the door and grab my things and leave the room. Jasmine stands in the living room with her bags and cries. In her arms, she has our one little sister Amanda, the other two, Oliver and Sandra are each lying on a blanket on the floor among diaper packages, and bags.

One of the social workers approaches me and Jasmine and ask us to come with her. We take our things and go out to the minivan which is open in the yard. It's freezing outside with a lot of snow. The social workers and the police help us pack everything in the van and buckling up our younger siblings. Jasmine and I put on jackets, hats, and mittens. Finally, our mother comes out with Arnie. She locks the front door and asks us to get on the bus.

We get on the bus and it's very crowded in there because of all the packing. The social workers and the policemen get into their cars and back out of the yard. They drive off and we follow in our minivan. I ask our mother what has happened and where we are going, our mother just says that we are going to live somewhere else now. I ask if our father should come along, and she says no because he is "dangerous". I don't think she's very nice either. I feel sad that our father can't come along and think that he will be very lonely and sad when he comes home, and no one is there. I don't want him to feel so sad and alone and left out all the time. It kind of hurts the soul. I pinch the back of my hand hard to keep from crying and say nothing more for the entire journey.

After only about twenty minutes we arrive at the village where we go to primary school, it is about five kilometers from our home.The social workers and the police park at an apartment complex on the same street as the school. They show us to an apartment on the ground floor. You enter through a gate and continue through a corridor. The social workers open the door that is furthest to the left. Our steps echo in the stairwell, and I am amazed. I've only been in one apartment before and it was our grandmother's apartment, which is like a townhouse with its own entrance.

The apartment we will live in is tiny. It only has one bedroom and a living room. It's already furnished. Everything smells strange like cleaning agents and old sofas. In the bedroom there are two bunk beds, Jasmine, Arnie, and I will share a room. Our mother will sleep in the living room where there is a corner sofa and a sofa bed, a table, and a TV. The youngest children should sleep in their pram in the wardrobe that is big enough for the pram.

I help carry everything in together with Jasmine. The neighbors look at us through the windows and I hate it. In the apartment, everything feels strange. I wonder how people can live in such small boxes as I think apartments are and how the cupboards can be so empty and so clean, without mouse or rat droppings, spiders, and mold. In the kitchen there is a dining table with four chairs and there is a set of crockery in the last cabinet. Ugly beige curtains hang in the windows.

When everything is packed, the social workers sit down with us in the kitchen. The police say thank you and leave. The social workers tell us that this is a sheltered accommodation and that our father is not allowed there. He doesn't know we're there and he's not allowed to contact us. We are not allowed to tell anyone that we live there and if our father comes to school we have to go to a teacher or the principal.

I'm having a hard time putting everything together because nothing unusual had happened. I ask how long we will stay here, and they say they don't know. My mother quickly adds that we are not allowed to talk to our father if we see him, in the same false tone as before. It hurts inside when she says that because I don't like him being outside. In my eyes, he has done nothing to deserve it. I think our mother is stupid and unfair, so I leave the kitchen without another word and go to the room I now share with Arnie and Jasmine. I unpack my things and put them on one of the beds. Arnie and Jasmine have "called dibs" the top bunk on both bunkbeds, so I simply take a bottom bed. I have absolutely no desire to share a room with my siblings, I find them annoying and really stressful to be with.

We live in the apartment for about two months. The neighbors often complain about us, say we make too much noise and I think these neighbors should stop being so darn nosy and just go die or something. I don't like living there but I like the proximity to the school. Even though I hate the apartment and the neighbors, it's nice not having to walk all those kilometers to school. Our mother often has her lady friends visit and then they talk badly about our father, which I don't like at all.

Our mother does not take care of our youngest siblings very well, especially Oliver who is often left alone in the closet, no matter how much he cries. I usually sneak up to him and just hold his little hand and pat him, so he won't be so lonely and sad. Our mother scolds me the times she finds me standing by him and tells me that I am not his mother, and I should stop caring. I don't want to stop caring about him, so I keep sneaking in.

Jasmine mostly takes care of Amanda and Sandra; she doesn't like Oliver. She often tells me that I can take care of him because we are both useless. On those occasions I usually kick her legs or tell her she should kill herself. She cries every time and runs to our mother to tell her how mean and stupid I am. Our mother takes Jasmine's side and scolds me, calling me an evil child and that I might as well live with our father, because I probably wanted him to find us and kill us all. I get very offended and angry and reply that she should have left me behind when we were forced to move and that she is completely sick in the head and that she deserved to be beaten to death. This always leads to more scolding and me being punished and going without food a couple of times.

During the time we live in this accommodation, we meet our father once. Jasmine, Arnie, and I run into him outside the convenience store in the village. I don't dare say anything, but just wave gently. He looks very sad, and I feel extremely sorry for him. At the same time, I'm scared because I don't know what to say or do. My siblings get really scared and run home, I follow the siblings, but I also don't want to leave our father. I want to be with him but know I must go back to the apartment. I'm sad inside that I must leave him alone. Once at the apartment, Arnie and Jasmine have already told our mother that we have met our father and she ask me if he followed or if I revealed where we were. I say no and shrug because I don't care if he has followed or not.

A short while later I see our father in the yard outside the apartment. Our mother becomes hysterical and calls the police. Arnie and Jasmine also get hysterical.

I don't care, I just think they are over the top and stupid. The police are coming - they tell us that they have spoken to our father and that he had gone home again. Our mother immediately calls her friends and tells her story, Jasmine and Arnie talk about it for the rest of the day and I'm so sick of them all. I am accused of being "daddy's favorite" and that I probably wished he would find us and beat us to death. I don't answer it but ignore them as much as possible and just want to go back home. Go home to my dad, my room, my plants, and my things.

A week later, our mother says we are moving back home. Just like that. She says that she and our father have straightened it all out and that everything will be fine. I don't feel anything about this, but just pack my things immediately. Later that day we are all back home. I immediately lock myself in my room and am very happy to see that our father has taken care of my plants while we were away. I sit with them for a while, then I draw before I go to bed. I am very tired and very tense, listening intently and worried if something is about to happen.

As a child, you usually try to cooperate with the adults, even when it feels unfair and wrong. You are so at the mercy of those who are supposed to take care of you. Our parents' behavior resulted in us several times having to move to either our grandmother, temporary sheltered accommodation, or women's shelters. Once there were no available places left, our grandmother could not take us in and there was no place in a nearby women's shelter, so Child Protective Service's simply placed us at a preschool for a weekend. They got keys and alarm codes to the preschool premises and let us in.

It was a bit more fun than the other options; it became a bit more like being on an adventure or a camp. We got to sleep on the preschoolers' soft rest mattresses, my younger siblings could play with a lot of toys, and we had an entire playground at our disposal for the entire seventy-two hours. At the same time, it felt embarrassing and strange to live in a preschool, in the middle of a small town where people around could see us and ask what we were doing there.

I've always had a hard time appreciating the company of strangers, I especially dislike strangers who stare, point, and talk loudly about you, as if you weren't there or as if you were an animal in a zoo. I dislike that kind of attention and loathe snooping people. Living at a preschool in a small town attracts attention and it attracts all the snooping people. Therefore, I mostly kept to myself during the short time we lived there. I also hated the times we lived in women's shelters. Partly it wasn't home, partly I just thought that the people who lived there were just sitting around feeling sorry for themselves and wallowing in their experiences.

The people who worked there, only felt sorry for the residents, from my point of view. They saw the men who hit, as "monsters", as "evil" and "horrible" and I could not agree with them. My father was neither a horrible monster nor evil, if so, my mother was an equally horrible and evil monster. Everyone should be judged fairly for their part in the violence, which I aired from time to time.

My understanding was that no one else there agreed with me, which only strengthened my belief that they were all stupid and delusional. They saw monsters and horrible violent men, I saw fathers who were alone and outside, just as I perceived my own father. I understand today that not all men who become aggressive and violent are alone or feel left out, but they all have different reasons for behaving the way they do. Some have such severe personality disorders and have such skewed ideas about other people and women in particular, that they should be incarcerated in mental institutions.

Although there are deeply disturbed men, the conviction remains that the vast majority of these men who beat women are not mentally disturbed monsters, but they are just as hurt by life as their partners have been, otherwise they would not have behaved the way they do. Again, that's not an excuse, there are no excuses for domestic violence or to stay in such a relationship, but I believe that there are reasons and explanations. Reasons and explanations should never be seen as excuses.

CHAPTER SIX

Living in our household was not always suffering and pain. Sometimes we had fun together. Unfortunately, these occasions are as rare as pink diamonds, but they were and are still there. Despite everything. And I have many times chosen to focus only on these little glimpses of joy.

Anyway, being at home usually meant conflicts and hard work, even for us children. We learned early on to wash, cook, clean, and take care of our younger siblings, the animals, and the garden. We had a cleaning schedule that we were expected to follow every week where we - meaning me and Jasmine - would clean half the house each. Half the house meant cleaning five out of a total of ten rooms, including doing laundry, dishes and feeding animals (we lived on a farm and kept cows, pigs, goats, chickens, and horses for a couple of years).

In addition to this, there was also mowing the grass, clearing weeds, repainting the house when needed and shoveling snow in the winter. Our mother simply just set up a schedule and we were not allowed to question, only execute. In return, we received a monthly allowance. Jasmine got one hundred and fifty SEK more than me because she was the oldest. In total, I earned three hundred and fifty SEK in one month and that money would be used for clothes, hygiene items and any entertainment for the next month.

Our mother never spent anything on us, beyond our monthly allowance except for food, electricity, and water. If we didn't do the job well enough, we got either less or no money at all that month. She took careful notes after each week's work supervision and kept a close eye on who had done exactly how much.

In Sweden we have something called government child support, it's a sum of money that parents get for each child they have in their care. Back in the day it was about 950 SEK per child. Which meant our parents, or our mother, got 6 650 SEK in governmental child support each month for all of us seven children.

I had no idea what governmental child support was for, nor the existence of governmental student grant for children aged sixteen to twenty-one. This was before the home computer and the Internet, so I couldn't look things up without going to the library or asking an adult.

Since I didn't know what governmental student grant or child support was and didn't think much about it, it wasn't something I felt I needed to research more about either. I learned exactly what these concepts were when I was placed in foster care as a seventeen-year-old and received the student grant myself. By then the home computer and the Internet had begun to be established in homes and my family was quick to catch on to the trend, but there was still nothing that raised questions for me and therefore it was still nothing that I questioned. Imagine my surprise when I realized that I had been entitled to this money long before I was placed in foster care!

I seriously believed that the governmental child support and later student grant my classmates were talking about was something their families had applied for and that was why they had more money than me. Never that I thought my parents got the same money! My mother had total control of all the money in the household, including my father's money that he transferred to their joint house account. Unfortunately, she was not the world's best manager of this money. We had large debts to the bailiff and were always short of healthy foods and clothes of the right size, which fits well with the rest of the dysfunctionality in the home.

Where exactly all that money went, only my mother knows, but I have understood it to mean that there were a lot of expensive purchases for herself, and she was often out partying on the weekends. My father used part of his money to support his alcohol addiction, but he was also thrifty and did not like to waste money except on the bare necessities. In retrospect, I understand that many people associate alcoholics with homelessness, outcasts, and other people in vulnerable social environments. Few imagine that someone can be a violent alcoholic and still have a savings account and hold a job. But my father made it work somehow. My father had the same job for over twenty years and hardly missed a day. He may not have been completely sober when he left for work in the morning, but he didn't drink alcohol until he got home. He didn't use up all his money on liquor and beer, but he also set aside a large portion for savings, apart from what was transferred to the house account.

Although he was a thrifty person, he was not one to ask for money anyway. He was happy to contribute a penny now and then, but you didn't want to end up on his "bad list", among people he despised and thus accused of being parasites, bloodsuckers, and exploiters. It was frighteningly easy to end up on that list if you didn't play your cards right, which meant being incredibly grateful and humble before the accepting his contribution or asking for money, taking his side in conflicts and being loyal in every imaginable situation. He could be extremely generous one day and shower someone with money and small gifts only to three days later aggressively accuse someone of stealing his money, taking advantage of his kindness and get really angry if you didn't realize he was the one who had hidden a gift inside in one's room or put it somewhere in the home without anyone knowing about it. It was expected that one would have knowledge and insight that there was a gift hidden in a large house, without having received any warning or prior information about it. You were just assumed to know about it and assumed to know who it was from, even if it wasn't written anywhere. Not even with invisible ink.

The demands and expectations were completely unreasonable at times, and it was very stressful trying to figure out what was valid for the given moment. My parents were also ones who took back gifts such as birthday presents or Christmas presents if they felt we would no longer have them, or if they felt these gifts could be given away to someone else (usually because they had forgotten to buy something for a cousin or friend's child). My mother sold all my toys to one of her friends when she thought I was too old to play with toys. I was eleven at the time and managed to smuggle out my dinosaur collection and a few other things. The rest, whether they were past Christmas gifts, birthday presents or if I had bought it myself, was mercilessly sold.

Sometimes our things were just given away or exchanged for other things that our mother wanted. Our dad wasn't as active in taking back or selling our things, but he could smash them to pieces if he felt like it. Alternatively, blast them with the shotgun or soft air gun we had at home and then promise it was our turn to be shot next time if we didn't behave better. So, the thing about receiving gifts and being able to keep gifts is not obvious to me, nor to my siblings. This has left its mark and even today I either get suspicious if I receive a gift or become so grateful that you notice that the other person thinks it is a little too grateful. It gets kind of too much. It is difficult to be "properly" grateful and refrain from asking probing questions about what the catch is, what are you expected to do if you accept the gift? Those who don't understand where you're coming from can be offended or confused or both when you question the gift or promise them recklessly ridiculous loyalty, like selling your soul.

At my work, we employees receive gifts for various holidays such as Easter or Christmas. The first few years I went to the boss and gave the gifts back, I really thought she had accidentally put the presents in the wrong place. They could never be meant for me, who did such a bad job and who was just an "imposter". Even my own grandmother didn't give me presents at Christmas or on birthdays from time to time, because she didn't think I deserved it. My later future partner, Gunnar, also used the thing about "deserving" gifts and could tell about a gift he intended to buy or a gift he had bought, and inform that if he thought that you had not "deserved" the gift, he would take it back. So why would my boss give gifts, without counter-demands or without directly deserving it?

This manager has had to explain many times that the gift was for me, just like for the other employees. Then I have asked why? What's the deal? Is anything expected of me in return? Nowadays she always writes my name on any gifts and goes inside my office to be clear that the gift is for me, and nothing is expected beyond my normal work tasks before she hurriedly goes back to her office. Still, I wrestle with anxiety and doubt because what if they're lying or playing tricks on me? A good aspect of that form of upbringing, where you can never count on keeping anything, neither stuff nor life, is that you learn not to get too attached to stuff.

There are probably those who become far too attached to the gadgets after such an upbringing and find it difficult to get rid of them. For me, gadgets mean stress, anxiety, and something you have to "guard" otherwise they disappear, so it's easier not to have so many things. Less stress and less anxiety. I expect to have to leave everything at some point, that nothing is permanent, and things are just things. Of course, I would miss certain things that have an emotional value to me, such as photos and memories, if these were to disappear in a fire, theft, or natural disaster. But I know I can miss the stuff and still live without it, just like with most of the people I've left behind to move forward. I may miss certain people, but I can live without them, even though it hurts not to have them in my life anymore.

CHAPTER SEVEN

Notes from therapy:

"I am seventeen years old, and it is spring with sun and warmth. It's a Saturday and I'm going to move in with a woman who is my friend Elin's aunt Veronica. The decision has been made by Social Services that I will live with Veronica. I have packed everything I own - it fits in two moving boxes. I'm nervous and sad because I know I won't be able to help my siblings in the same way anymore. My older sister Jasmine is terribly angry with me for moving. She screams and yells that I think I'm someone, that I'm an idiot and a dumbass who has told social services what it's like at home. She screams that I'm never ever welcome back home again.

Our father helps me carry my desk and my two boxes out to the car. He has supported me in this and says that it is good that at least someone gets away from there. I can tell he's sad but doesn't say much. I feel mostly empty and numb inside. My younger siblings are worried and look out their bedroom windows facing the courtyard. They don't dare go out. Our mother is going to drive me to Veronica, and she is not happy at all, but she pretends to be okay with the move. In fact, she is very angry, and she points out several times that this is the last time I will see my siblings, because they will never be allowed to visit someone like me, and I am not welcome back home.

I'm sad but doesn't show any emotions. It hurts incredibly to leave my younger siblings, but I hope they too get help soon (unfortunately they don't). I jump into the car and our mother drives to the town where I will be moving. All the time she talks in a fake friendly manner, and I don't feel safe. I'm sure she'll freak out at any moment and just dump me and my stuff at the side of the road. I have a big lump of anxiety in my stomach, and I feel like I'm letting everyone down and that I've done something fundamentally wrong or stupid.

My mother drives me to the parking lot outside Veronica's apartment and leaves the car idling. She demonstratively sits in the car and lets me unpack the car myself. When everything is relieved in the parking lot, she looks at me both pleading and accusing from the driver's seat, with the window nervous. She says "have a good time, then", then she backs out of the parking lot and drives away.

I can't stand in the parking lot because everything feels very difficult and hard. I want to cry but I hold myself together. I grab a box and walk towards Veronica's apartment which is a bit away, but thankfully on the ground floor. I knock gently on the door, terrified that everything has gone wrong and that maybe I won't live there at all after all. I'm thinking about whether I should stay with Paulina or Elin in that case, until everything is set right again. Veronica opens the door and seems happy to see me. We have only met once before together with the Social Services when they made a suitability assessment.

Veronica takes my box and asks me to come in. She gets angry when she realizes that my parents are not going to help more than they have, that my mother has just dumped me and my things in a parking lot. She calls her sister Karin, who is Elin's mother, and asks her to come over and help. Soon Karin, Elin and her sister Jessica will come over and help carry in and set up my room.

I'm always very, very grateful but also very, very scared, and insecure. I miss my siblings and hope they are doing well. I sleep restlessly at night, trying to settle into a new home, a new bed, new smells and new sounds."

It all started after a teacher encouraged me to talk to the school counsellor. My friends Paulina and Elin had expressed concern for me to our PE teacher. They suspected that I wasn't doing so well at home and that I might have an eating disorder (both of which were true, but nothing I had told them about). The PE teacher asked to talk to me and asked how I was really doing. Vaguely I told a little about how it might be a little difficult at home sometimes with fights and arguing and yes, maybe I thought I was fat and ugly and disgusting. So, he encouraged me to talk to the school counselor.

I had never talked to a school counsellor before, avoiding them like the plague because I knew they could "mess it up" for my family if I revealed something. But in the conversation, I finally told them about what life was like at home, about how my siblings and I suffered and how our parents were not always very kind to us. The school counsellor phoned in a report of concern to Child Protective Services, with me in the room. Before I left the room, I was given a time and a day to visit the social services office alone, secretly.

There, in that meeting, I was incredibly nervous, I was alone and there were several social service administrators at a large table. The whole thing was extremely frightening. And since most of my siblings and I weren't allowed to use the shower at home, I hadn't showered for a week. My hair was stripy, and I probably didn't smell that well. That's how I showed up at the meeting with the Child Protective Services. They asked about my appearance, and I told them everything. The food- and water- restrictions, the bathroom restrictions and the shower/bath-ban regarding me and my siblings. I also mentioned the continuously fighting, the arguing, my father's drinking, and my mother's abuse of medication, as well as my younger siblings being forced to wear diapers well above the need for it, only because our mother gained government aid for my siblings' "incontinence", which was only caused due to the restricted access to the restroom. After the meeting, it was decided to place me in a foster home. I thought my siblings would get help too, from this meeting. Oh, how wrong I was.

Two weeks later, I moved to Veronica and lived there until I moved in with Carl. In the time from when I moved away from home until today, the contradictions within the family grew exponentially. At home, my younger siblings were told that they were not allowed to see me anymore, they were told that I abandoned them, that I abandoned the whole family. I was no longer "one of them". I became an "outsider".

Children are very adaptable. You learn to adapt to your surroundings, and you learn to accept and tolerate, even expect a certain treatment. You absorb what you see and hear, even if it hurts and even if you don't always understand what's going on. My younger siblings were at this time in middle school, they had lived their whole lives within the framework of what our parents could give. As a child, you love your parents unconditionally and you put up with the most disgusting situations and the most brutal actions, only to maybe, hopefully be loved and accepted back.

My younger siblings often sneaked to my new home during school breaks, scared and anxious about maybe being caught. I loved the moments they came by. But then, our mother and Jasmine had learned about their visits to me and suddenly they disappeared from my life again. I was not welcome home, and I was not welcome to contact any of my siblings. I was only allowed to be in touch with our father.

I think this limitation, this control of my siblings' contact with me and the lies they were told about me "abandoning" them, at the beginning of my new life, is part of the reasons why we are so estranged today. We didn't have any cohesion before, we were just there at the mercy of the life we had. A life filled with control, the exercise of power, punishments, separation, and divisions. When I was taken into foster care, I thought that they would get help too, which unfortunately they didn't and this, together with the family culture they were allowed to remain in, is probably the breeding ground from which their future disgust towards me was founded.

There are times when we have tried to reconnect, but most often it falls back into old ruts again. These ruts mean that we talk on a couple of occasions or send a couple of text messages, and then let the contact die out. During a psychologist session, the psychologist asked me at one point if we siblings ever meet just to have lunch, go for a walk, or just hang out as siblings. These occasions can be counted on one hand and then it has been that we have met at our father's house or that it has been a holiday. It has never happened that any of us siblings have even thought of asking another if we should "have lunch together" or hang out. That idea is as foreign to all of us as eating manure.

Despite our estrangement from each other, my opinion is that it is usually me who tried to keep the contact between me and my siblings. However, it didn't take long before my siblings stop responding and become evasive. They avoid my text messages, my phone calls and pretend not to see me if we meet in town. They can socialize with each other, not to have lunch or just hang out, but because it is a requirement between them. I know it's a requirement, because the siblings I've talked to have expressed it as just that, that you *SHOULD* meet, just because. Nothing else. No lunch plans, no movie nights, you just have to sit in the same room and pretend to like each other's company just because you are siblings.

In a way, I could try to be involved in it, but I think the conditions for being allowed to "be involved" are too high. In that case, I need to sacrifice my values, principles and integrity and I am not willing to do so again. There was a period when I had no principles, values, or integrity. I wasn't aware of what these concepts were, or how to set boundaries. This meant that I behaved much like my siblings and our parents, but without the addiction. I have strictly stayed away from alcohol, drugs, and pills. I also don't use any violence since I turned twelve, and I don't like to verbally abuse anyone else, even though when I was a child, I was very adept at verbally insulting Jasmine and Arnie, both of whom were my biggest annoyances.

On the other hand, I have played along with all my siblings' games and gossiped, slandered, and recklessly criticized both one and the other, based on who said what and who I would be allowed to "belong to", if only for a short moment. I willingly threw everything and everyone in the family under the bus to get a bit of community, knowing that I was the one who would get the slander next time. That's just the way it was. Today I don't feel good in such situations. It crawls under my skin, and I never know what to talk about. So, I'd rather not do it and stay away. I really don't want to be lured into that behavior again, it's so destructive and unhealthy and nothing I want to invest in anymore. I can talk about abuses, about inequality and about the dysfunctionality we grew up in, but the intention comes out of a desire and a drive to try to create understanding and acceptance of what has been.

No trash-talk, no slander, just to discuss the situation. The criterion for this kind of conversation is that I need to do what I can to understand the other person. To realize that I don't have all the answers, I don't know everything and I'm the reference point in other people's lives. This book is, as mentioned before, an aid for me to understand and a way to show others in similar situations, that everything really isn't black/white or good/evil, there are nuances to just about everything and that it can be good to try to understand why people do what they do instead of assuming or accusing. Sometimes you need to assume things, because you may not be able to get answers to certain questions, then you are at the mercy of assumptions. But then you can at least make as fair assumptions as possible, even if it is difficult and difficult.

There are countless times I have felt betrayed, hurt, and exploited by my siblings. Where I have assumed a lot about their doings and each other. They have guaranteed the same experiences of me, especially since they were told that I "opted out" when I moved, which was never true. Our family is and has always been very strongly polarized and divided into "cliques": for or against our father, for or against our mother, for or against me, for or against Oliver. The ones who controlled these "cliques" were our parents, Jasmine, and Arnie. Why Arnie and Jasmin have been so strong in their beliefs about who should "belong" to whom, I actually don't know. I have not yet come up with a good answer to that question.

When I moved away from home, it was easier for my parents and these two of my siblings to make me look like a betrayer, someone who doesn't care about the family, one who leaves others behind, rather than to see it as an opportunity for them to leave as well. I have understood that this is how it felt for them, that it was what they were told and learned at home, about Big Sister the Traitor, the Abandoner. She who disappeared to get a better life *without* them.

What they didn't know then, not until they were adults themselves, was that I always had hopes that they would also be relocated. I thought, with the report of concern that came in about me from school, that my siblings would also get help and support. Unfortunately, that help never came, and the explanation I received from the Child Protective Service's was that the report of concern only applied to me, not my siblings. For me, this was like a cold shower, because I had explicitly said that my siblings were abused, too. All those times the Child Protective Service's had been on home visits, all the investigations that had been started and then closed, all that should have made them realize that my siblings also needed help. But it was obviously not enough.

As an adult, both my sister Sandra and I have been told by a Child Protective Service's worker, who was working on our cases at the time, that the reason they were never did anything was partly that our parents declined to cooperate with them, and partly that there were so many of us children that it would be difficult for the social services to find new homes for all of us. So, they sacrificed all of us, especially my siblings. At least that's how I experienced it.

All of this was contained within the time before I learned that all events and situations you encounter in life are challenges and coincidences that you should learn from. It is not to "have bad luck in life" or to have "drawn a bad lottery ticket in life", life is not a thing that just happens. Life and all the experiences it contains, are something you have chosen in one way or another, even the most painful experiences. Before I learned this, I had to go through several painful situations. With the huge gap that existed and remains among most of my siblings, there is also an abysmal pain among my siblings. It has been an endless pain inside me that my siblings had to grow up with the idea that I didn't care about them, that I abandoned them. When I have explained my siblings' actions and behavior towards me to my psychologist, they described it as sounding like these siblings are angry with me. Which is probably quite true.

I know how angry and upset I've been at everything and everyone who I think has abandoned me. So, I think it's reasonable that my siblings feel that way, with the information they have that I abandoned them. This pain has manifested itself in the fact that my sisters Jasmine and Amanda in particular have deliberately tried to hurt me by saying the most absurd and strange things. Like I'm trying to "control" them through Social Services and social media, even though I haven't had any contact with any of them for several years. Or all the times Jasmine and Sandra have sent abusive and threatening text messages, hoping that I will react, which I honestly did the first few years, before I learned that it is better to just not answer such text messages or calls. Or that Amanda, Jasmine, Sandra, and Oliver withheld our father's cancer diagnosis because they held the idea that I shouldn't care. Not that I *did* care or *didn't* care, but that I, according to them, *didn't have the right to care.* According to their learned behavior, the same behavior I also had when I was younger, was, as mentioned earlier, to be there no matter what you must endure. It is the same as being loving and caring. Since I had put my foot down for some time and not agreed to be offended and abused anymore, they simply assumed that I no longer loved our father. Likewise, when I changed to another surname and thus no longer bore our father's surname, it was interpreted as me abandoning our father on paper as well.

Today, with more maturity and a different approach, it feels completely absurd to write out the above, because it is an absurd assumption to assume that you no longer love someone just because you set healthy boundaries or that you abandon someone just because you change your last name.

Names and healthy boundaries have nothing to do with hate, love or abandonment, most people understand that, but that's the logic I grew up with, as well as my siblings. If I hadn't mentally grown up, because of that absurd logic that flows within my family of origin, I would have tried to figure out what I had done wrong and what I should do to correct it, especially if accusations and rumors were directed at me. I would have fallen back into learned patterns of behavior and tried to please everyone, and sort things out, react to everything as if it were personal, and be submissive and compliant. I would also have behaved offended and angry and said a lot of mean things to them and about them.

But over the years, I have considered these situations with a little more compassion, both to myself and to my siblings and our parents. It took quite a while to get there. The road to compassion has been tortuous, full of pitfalls and missteps. It has not been entirely easy to walk this path. I've found it easier to just dismiss people and their feelings than to try to accept them as they are and even harder not to take things personally. I need to remind myself from time to time that they are just as lost as I once was and as a part of me still is. They probably don't have it as easy as adults and I know that none of them have had it easy either before, or after my move to a foster family.

An outsider once accused me of being too passive towards my siblings when they have chosen to either openly hate and smear my name on social media or avoid me as if I was the plague itself. Sure, I'm passive, but I don't believe in forcing myself into someone else's life and I don't believe in trying to counter-argue their expressed hatred and slander. I would rather leave them alone, there will be less conflicts and it is better for all parties, according to me. The experiences they have had taught them to behave the way they do, and I can't force them to change or start thinking in new directions.

All my siblings have been or are confused, so absorbed in everything that has happened or not happened in their lives that right now they don't have the ability to stop and reflect on what lives they have created. They are rootless, ungrounded, and fragmented in themselves. The reason I know that is that I have been there myself. I have been rootless, ungrounded, and divided. I have burned bridges, slandered, talked ill, turned my coat to the wind, lied to myself and others and taken sides. I have tried to embellish the circumstances I have tried to appear better than others. I've lied about how I feel, how I'm doing, how much or how little I've done or how good I am at something. I have broken trusts, I have stuck to rigid opinions about this and that and when I have been exposed, I have tried to blame others or circumstances.

I have tried to be and think like those I have spent time with or who meant something to me, like my father and those of my siblings who have taken his side. I have put on opinions, thoughts, feelings, and prejudices that have not been mine, but those of others and I have been extremely afraid of being rejected, offended, or abused. I have sacrificed myself, my dignity, my self-respect, and my boundaries to please others, because that was what was taught within the family. I've done almost everything to be allowed belonging, to be involved, to experience some kind of community and what I've always thought was love. Who am I to blame them for their behavior, when I know what they have been taught?

My siblings are where I was just a couple of years ago. It's better to give them time and space to find their own path and come to terms with things through age-appropriate maturity. So instead of reacting to their behaviors, as I did before, I think it's better to be patient and forgiving and thus passive. They have the right to be who they are, and it is my duty to let them be who they are, just as I want them to let me be who I am, in my way. Just because I have reached a certain maturity or come to certain realizations, it is not certain that "my path" is right for them or that they need the same "maturity" as I do. After all, we are different people with different life choices. There is no miracle cure that suits every single person. They are free to create the lives they want with all that these lives contain. Life takes time, quite simply.

CHAPTER EIGHT

"When your life goes downhill, it won't get better just because you want to. It also won't get better just because you think it should be better. Your life only gets better when you take better care of it yourself." –
Iyanla Vanzant

It would take several years before at least my life got better. In the meantime, I tried to make life better with what little I had. It was like trying to fix a broken airplane with duct tape. It might be possible, but it won't be good. Something will come loose eventually and it's a hell of a job to keep track of all the parts being taped on. It takes a lot of energy to pretend that you are not taped together at all, but that you are unharmed and free of scratches, holes, or missing pieces. Camouflaging everything is not sustainable in the long run, not even for a professional military. Sooner or later, things come out in their true nature.

For my part, I tried to pretend that I was not influenced by my parents' behavior or choice of upbringing. I've pretended that it wasn't anything special or meant anything, when in fact it affected my brain structure and thus my way of relating to things. Such things as how I relate to other people, other people's sufferings and to spirituality. All these are areas that have often been questioned by others. Like how can I be unmoved by listening to stories about the suffering of others? How can I not be upset when injustices are happening around the world? And how can I believe in a higher power, when I have lived through what I have lived through?

I can only answer that by having lived through what I have lived through, I am not as affected by the sufferings of others, nor am I directly upset by different kinds of human injustices. My experiences tell me that life is just as fair as you make it out to be and sometimes life is deeply unfair. It's something you have to accept that that's the way it is. But that doesn't mean I don't want to see changes and it doesn't mean I ignore others. I would like children, women, Sami, Swedish Finns, Roma, Pakistanis, Syrians and all other vulnerable groups to be seen as equal people in all parts of society. I would like to see an end to oppression, violence, and racism. I want the rainforest to be preserved and environmental degradation to stop. But I realize that this is the way life looks on this planet at the moment, I just have to accept that. Many people think that if you accept something, you automatically agree with what is happening, which is a wrong assumption. Acceptance is not about agreeing with or liking what is happening. Acceptance is about seeing reality as it is, no matter how it is, and not getting emotionally destroyed for every little thing.

I've been in that situation already, where everything upset me, where "justice" was played out as extremely violent mini-movies in my imagination. I fantasized about punishing and exterminating all the "horrible, evil people" that are out there, those who rape children, burn forests, and enslave people. Those who create war, destroy, and poison the environment. But my spiritual perception has always prevented me from living out these fantasies and seeing it as it is; fantasies that cannot or should not be lived out. My relationship with the Creator and nature is and has always been a very important part of my life and it is not my or anyone else's right to decide over the lives of others or how those lives should be lived.

Neither of my parents were religious, but I developed a deep relationship with the Creator early on. As far back as I can remember, I prayed to the Creator every night. I prayed that my parents would stop fighting and that they wouldn't die. I was terrified that they would die during the night, or that I would die during the night and not have the ability to "save" my family from some unknown danger lurking around the corner. I prayed that nature would be saved and that all the animals and plants would have peace.

I perceived the concept of the Creator, when I was a child, as something "outside" myself, something invisible, but tangible that existed in everything in nature and in the air. Therefore, I could sometimes also talk to trees, animals, and plants, they were and are as much the Creator as Jesus was the Creator's son. The deity that was written in the Old Testament… that one I have a hard time with, I never bought the story of an old white man in heaven, it felt wrong. Likewise, about an "Almighty Father" who is thoroughly masculine and judgmental and who one should watch out for. I have never liked that form of scaremongering. The Deity mentioned in the New Testament is closer to my concept of the Creator, but not as a physical or non-physical being pulling all the strings. The Creator for me is an intricate system made up of energy that permeates everything and everyone. A kind of field of consciousness that we are all part of and that we can influence with our senses because we are all part of this field.

In my early childhood years, I talked to the Creator as a kind of being *outside of* me because I had such a hard time internalizing that I too could be a part of this Creation. Everyone else was, of course, but I was so marinated in self-loathing even then, that I could not bring myself to count myself in the Creator's children's group. Talking to the Creator was something I absolutely did not share with anyone else. To be a believer was and still is today absolutely nothing that any of my relatives "approve of". They despise religion and spirituality, Christianity, and Islam in particular. They are of the opinion that either there is no

Creator because no one has ever seen this Creator. Or, if there is a Creator, then it is not a kind being because we have had the upbringing we have had. That is the view I suspect many others also have: that how can you, who have the experiences you have, believe in the Creator? My father was of that opinion and believed that if you face adversity in life, if life is difficult and unfair, it is because the Creator is unjust and terrible. Thus, there can be no Creator.

For my part, I believe I have the experiences I have, precisely because the Creator exists. My experiences must have a meaning, otherwise it quickly becomes very painful to be human and it goes against my beliefs. I don't think that humans are meant to live in spiritual pain really, but it's something we humans have created for ourselves, and I think we all have predetermined experiences that we need to learn from, that's why we create the lives we have. As a child, it was hard to see it that way, but the older I get, the more I understand, even though I will probably never fully understand things. I am convinced that we all carry the experiences of previous generations with us in our DNA and that it comes out in different ways in the lives we live today. Not to make things difficult for us, but simply to relieve us of the pain, by making the wounds visible. When we feel the wounds, it is our job to heal them. The generational pain of my family's ancestors is on my siblings and me and our children and grandchildren to heal. It gives me a comforting feeling to perceive it that way.

When I was little, I had no idea about the long generations of priests and church ministers we had in the family. Nor was there any talk about spirituality, spirituality and talking to nature, which is very close in the family via the Sami and Finnish roots we have. Faith has always been like a comforting light in the darkness. I thought it was a nice feeling, that inner light. When I felt the most abandoned, it was always there to comfort me, even though I didn't think I deserved it.

This light sometimes took a physical form as a ball of light that floated in the room when I was going to sleep, especially when I was extra worried and stressed. Likewise, this ball of light was with me all the dark winter days I walked to and from school, the several kilometers on the country roads without streetlights. If I were to describe the Light, the closest, and then not complete, description would be a sphere of different colors, such as green, amber, gold, silver, pink, purple, yellow that hovered with an inner light that illuminated all other shades and colors. It radiated a calm and a security that I could not and still cannot put into words. The light was sometimes my only company and sometimes it was in the company of Jasmine who sometimes seemed to see the same as me and sometimes not.

However, it has not always been obvious to practice my faith, nor has there been a straight line to follow. At one point in my life, during my teenage years and early adulthood, I didn't feel this light, nor did I have as good a "connection" with my faith. At times I have been so busy trying to find a place, somewhere to belong, and have then unconsciously searched for belonging and fellowship with others and then temporarily forgotten my spiritual convictions. There have been periods where I have doubted, allowed myself to be convinced otherwise, followed other values and other ideas. During that period, I got really lost, recreated the dysfunctional patterns I had been taught, and walked on different paths. Listened to everyone else except myself and the Creator. Towards the end of the relationship, I had then started with a narcissistic so-called "healer", I found the light again, or rather, it made sure that I found it. After I had new experiences that were difficult to accept and digest.

CHAPTER NINE

There was a time when I was blinded and limited in what I thought was love, and I thought that was how love would be. I was stuck in my own dysfunctional cycle. My frames of reference about what was a healthy relationship were skewed, distorted by the environment I had grown up in. When I was seventeen years old and was at my internship and was love bombed by the man who was the owner of the store, I had no idea that it was wrong and highly inappropriate.

Carl, a forty-seven-year-old heavy smoker, alcoholic, and with bad breath, was not exactly attractive at all. But he was charming, showered me with gifts, compliments and invited me on a trip to Denmark to make purchases for the store. We quickly became a couple, despite the big age difference. My parents (the grooming started slightly before I was placed in foster care) and other relatives did not have any objections and if they did, they didn't say anything to me, and no one prevented me from having a relationship with him. I was an emotionally very vulnerable person, yet or because of it, he was willing or desired a relationship with me. The fact that he already had a girlfriend, Annica, who was only a couple of years older than I was, was something he explained by the fact that they had broken up but that she hadn't found a home of her own yet, so she was more of a lodger than his girlfriend. Her presence in his life was only a trifle, something that would soon be removed.

In the meantime, he explained, it was important that we keep quiet about our relationship so that she wouldn't find out about it, because she was apparently morbidly jealous and would become very violent. If you're a lost, dysfunctional teenager with no frame of reference whatsoever about what constitutes a healthy relationship and what are clear red flags, you're easy to deceive and manipulate. I was no exception. So, we had a "secret" relationship for a little more than a year. Carl was the first person who made me feel seen and validated. He had made me tell him a little about my childhood, and I know today that he used it to manipulate me, like the abuser he was.

Carl pointed out several times that all secrecy was for "our good", that I had to trust his judgment because otherwise I would ruin his life, just as I ruined my siblings' lives by telling outsiders about our home life. During that time, Carl groomed me with travel, gifts, clothes, compliments and all the "love" I had never received. These were completely new experiences for me. Carl was the first man who approached me, who seemed to like me. We talked several times every day, he drove all the way to my foster home to meet me. He noticed my curiosity about spirituality and spiritualism and talked far and wide about things I so wanted to know. He said that he was a great spiritual leader, a "chosen" healer, and I would be his "disciple." In my head, this meant that he accepted me and loved me. He was somewhere my fantasy of the love, acceptance and belonging I lacked so much in my life, and I fell headlong for that fantasy.

Shortly after I turned eighteen, Carl persuaded me to give my virginity to him on the toilet floor at his workplace. I was very insecure and hesitant. He was sure of his cause and commanding. I didn't find the courage to say no, afraid of losing this fellowship with someone, so I let him do whatever he wanted.

Afterwards, I quickly repressed the event, put it in a dark corner in my innermost being. Several such events took place during the years after.

Also, he arranged for me to live in a small room in an industrial area where he rented a room of ten square meters. There, in his new little shop, I had to live for a couple of months under the pretext that his "roommate" wouldn't go crazy with jealousy and commit suicide. She was "too fragile to handle the truth", as he said. So, it was best the way it was at the time. I didn't want to have on my conscience that she would kill herself, because of me. I had this guilt and fear with me from childhood. I really believed that what was being told to me was the truth. I had experienced it with my own eyes several times, that others could really try to kill themselves because I was stupid and wrong. So, for me, it was obvious that if it happened, it was of course my fault. Therefore, I had to behave well and obey Carl, just as I had previously tried to behave and obey my family. I had admittedly been taken care of in a way, but my learned emotional and behavioral pattern was still there, almost unchanged.

After a couple of months in the cold and scary premises, he was forced to move me because other shop tenants suspected that I lived there permanently, which was against the law. After all, it was industrial premises, not residential premises. The complaints made him find a home in the same village where he lived, a collective that I was unhappy in. I have never liked living with many people, strangers on top of that. The fact that I didn't arrange a home myself or tell my parents how it was because Carl was so convincing in that he – and only he - could find the right home for me. After all, I came from a small town, several miles away, and he knew several different premises and subletting companies in this bigger town. I only had the study grant as income when I studied art at a public adult high school. I didn't want my parents to know anything, I was afraid of being criticized and mocked for my ignorance in the big city. So, I kept quiet and trusted Carl.

After a couple of months in the collective, the whole secrecy ended. I was at his house one night and by now I knew that he expected me to be with him sexually. If I didn't, I was told how ungrateful I was and for everything he had done for me, I basically owed him to have sex with him. This evening, as on many other evenings, his "roommate" was out of town - he thought. So, after "thanking" him for his "goodness" in his bedroom, he suddenly ran up from the bed. He yelled at me to go upstairs immediately. I didn't even have time to get any clothes on, but he pushed me up the stairs to the second floor and locked me in a small room. There I tried to understand what was going on and find something to cover myself with. I found a blanket in a corner and wrapped it around my body. Then I just had to wait for him to let me out again. My body trembled from the stress, and I tried to push away the creeping panic. I have a really hard time with tight spaces and small rooms, especially when I'm trapped and have a hard time getting out. In retrospect, I realize that I could have climbed out of the window, but that thought didn't occur to me at that moment. I was paralyzed by stress, fear, and anxiety.

From the kitchen downstairs there were angry voices, someone screaming and yelling. Porcelain that flew to the floor. Then I heard footsteps on the stairs and the door opened. Carl looked annoyed and asked me to come downstairs. I asked what was happening and if I could get something to wear. I didn't get an answer to any of the questions and didn't dare to go to get clothes. With the adrenaline pumping in my body, I went down to the kitchen, dressed only in a blanket.

In the kitchen stood a terribly angry person. I didn't understand who it was, I had never met her before. She pushed me and yelled that I was a whore. Then I understood that she was Carl's so-called "roommate" and then she really did reason to be called crazy, because she looked crazy, and she behaved like a crazy person. I was nineteen years old, had only just finished high school and I was terrified and ashamed of my nakedness where I stood in just a blanket.

I asked Carl several times to be allowed to put on clothes, but neither he nor his now apparently former girlfriend let me go and get any clothes. Instead, they pushed me down into a kitchen chair and Annica, as this hysterically crazy woman was called, demanded to know all the details about Carl's and my relationship. I answered as best I could, and Carl "corrected" me on the points where he would otherwise have appeared as an unfaithful jerk. For him, it was important that his reputation was spotless, this was Annica's and my fault. Not his. If Annica hadn't been so crazy and didn't understand that they had broken up (according to his statement) and if I hadn't been so lovesick, none of us would have ended up in this situation. I believed in him. It sounds crazy, but I believed him.

It sounded true, what he said and in my skewed world of thought, that was probably how it was, even if it chafed a little inside that Carl would come out of the conflict that had arisen "flawlessly". I sensed a certain familiar pattern, and I denied it. However, it all worked out so that I eventually got to put on my clothes and was assigned to the small room upstairs while Carl and Annica "sorted out" their relationship. I didn't sleep all night, terrified of losing the community and belonging I thought I had with Carl. I was determined to keep this relationship, or rather what that relationship symbolized for me: to be allowed to belong somewhere, even if it was at the expense of myself.

CHAPTER TEN

True love usually doesn't look the way you've imagined it, nor is it the way you're taught in movies or through teenage magazines. One's own imagination and longing for love, strongly affects how one chooses one's relationships and how one chooses to behave in one's relationships. Love as taught by society, has the power to bring out all the unpleasant sides of all parties involved. Unfortunately, the problem is that this isn't love, but it's mistaken for it and that's the great danger.

The more I thought I loved Carl, the more disgusting I felt as a human being. More and more I felt unworthy of his love and his care. He was also not shy about pointing out that I should be grateful that he had even chosen me in the first place. He made me feel chosen one moment and unworthy the next. He started phasing out my friends, the very few I had, who were not "good enough" as my company. They had a "bad influence" on me, according to him. With sadness, I saw my childhood friend Paulina disappear. Wither away to nothing. Paulina herself chose to leave our relationship, as she thought I was disgusting to be with such a much older man. She brought many mutual acquaintances with her, much to Carl's delight. Only Elin saw it all as it was, and stood there through thick and thin, patiently waiting for me to see what she saw. To Carl's enormous annoyance. He tried several times to convince me to dump Elin, claiming that she was not good for me or for the relationship. Thankfully, I refused to listen to him on that point and fought to keep Elin in my life.

Though he couldn't phase out Elin, before I knew it, he had phased out all my clothes and jewelry and replaced them with ones that he had selected and approved. He phased out my records, my books, my interests, and many of my physical memories from childhood. I was no longer allowed to watch what movies I wanted, I was not allowed to paint or draw whatever I wanted, nor could I go to bed when I wanted. All attempts to defy him ended in heated arguments that always involved blaming me and accusing me of wanting to ruin his life.

Hadn't he "saved" me from my "terrible" parents perhaps? Hadn't he given me a roof over my head, jewelry, clothes? *Love?* Was this the thanks for his unselfish helpfulness, defying his wishes? Who did I think I was, really? Was I really *that* selfish and egocentric that I only cared about myself? These were his favorite questions, and he knew very well, that I had such deep insecurities about myself and really saw myself as unworthy and selfish. He simply took advantage of this, and I let him take advantage of me.

Sure, I had a hard time setting boundaries and speaking up because I had been taught to be compliant and submissive, but I still need to take responsibility for letting the situation be as it was because it was easiest that way. It was easier to put your life in the hands of someone else than to stand up for yourself and take responsibility for your life. So, that's what I did. Carl then decided on the passwords to email accounts, the PIN code for the phone and my payment card. All under explanations such as that he knew better, he wanted my best, he wanted to "protect me" from being exploited by others and from being manipulated by those around me who did not understand that he was a holy man, chosen by various Native American nations to represent them in Scandinavia. I was fortunate to be his wife and to have him as a guide in my life. He claimed. And I believed in him because he could really be convincing.I believed him, because if I didn't, I would be abandoned again.

In addition, I realize now in retrospect, I would have had to take responsibility for the life I had created. I wasn't ready for that at the time. Carl also decided which jobs I would apply for and which jobs I could have. All were within his domains in the municipality and in areas where he could exercise control. He knew who worked there, what they did and above all what I did. Studying at college or university, which was my dream since childhood, was just something that elitist right-wing populist fascists did. Not chosen spiritual people, so if I wanted to continue to be chosen, I had to give up that dream.

Higher studies were not something that honest and especially "spiritual" people did. It was dirty, undignified, contemptuous.Throughout this time, I felt more and more unworthy, dirty, and horrible. I didn't think I deserved his love, he was too good for me, in my twisted universe. This mental pain didn't really have much to do with him at all. I had no healthy frames of reference to go by. For me, a relationship where I was at least not physically beaten, was better than no relationship at all. What pained me was that I more often felt that I was not grateful enough for Carl, did not appreciate his kindness and care to the extent that he clearly deserved.

I was in a relationship with a great "spiritual leader", who had taken me as his "apprentice" and wanted to show me the way to "enlightenment". After all, Carl was well-known in spiritual circles, admired and liked by others. He had many contacts, both with politicians, municipal workers, and representatives of the Navajo and Lakota nations in the United States, as well as some Bolivian nations. He participated in various festivals, held courses and fundraisers. So why did I care so much about how much he drank or where our money went? Why did it bother me that he smoked indoors and never cleaned up after himself? Why did I find it so hard to understand that he deserved a couple of drinks and a bottle of wine after a strenuous day at work? Who was I to deny him relaxation and pleasure?

Why couldn't I appreciate him and his "grandiose generosity" in the same worshipful way as his "followers"? Why couldn't I see beyond the alcohol, the shattered economy and what it was like at home? Was I really that terrible? So destroyed by society, as Carl put it? At least he tried to make me have that opinion.

With Carl's approval, I took various simpler courses at a local school for adults, and worked as an hourly employee in the municipality, all under Carl's supervision. We got married in a private ceremony at home, in our garden. I was a little over twenty years old and he was over fifty years old. Even though it was my own wedding day, I was the one who had to cook all the food, set the table, clean, serve the guests and be a "worthy hostess". Carl's job was to entertain the guests and drink alcohol. Dressed in my wedding dress that I had had to make myself, and a cheap wedding ring from a market in Copenhagen, I rushed around and served. Carl sat with the guests, commanded me to do this or do that. He got so drunk that he passed out in the hallway at five in the morning. I was deeply disappointed in both him and myself.

The year after our wedding, we went to the United States. It was my first longer trip. We worked hard as volunteers on a Native American reservation. It was rewarding, challenging, and exhausting. Before this trip, I emailed a lot with Carl's good friend, Andrew Horseman, someone who would help us settle in on the reserve where his family lived. We got along well and after returning home Andrew and I kept in touch.

Back home in Sweden, life continued as usual, and I felt increasingly worse mentally and emotionally. After yet another fight over Carl's alcohol abuse and poor management of our money, he went to work, angry and offended. Before leaving, he had again pointed out how he had "saved" me and that I "owed" him my life and obliged to honor him. I was an ungrateful monster, a selfish bitch who couldn't appreciate everything he'd given me. He left our home and I decided to leave this life.

During the morning I took out all my bank papers, wrote down phone numbers for my parents and siblings, wrote down my social security number and codes to the bank, email, and phone. Carl had them, but if someone else were to find me before he came home, they had everything they needed to finish the administrative parts of my life here on earth.

I put everything on the kitchen table along with a note where I asked for forgiveness for being such a horrible person who didn't appreciate all the nice things Carl and others had done for me. My way of relieving them was to take my own life. After that I found a rope and tied a noose in a rafter. To test the durability of the rope, I jumped from the chair I was standing on while holding onto the noose in my hands. The rope did not hold. With tears in my throat and with a heightened sense of failure, I threw the now useless rope aside and went to find a new rope. Without finding one.

I couldn't even find a shoelace and was extremely angry with myself for this. I should have planned it all better. I realized that much of the morning had been spent, Carl would soon be home again, so I cleaned away everything I had picked up and started to cook lunch. The rest of the day and the years after, passed as if I hadn't tried to end my life.

Carl's and my relationship were the same as before. His choice of clothes, food, books, movies, socializing, working hours, studies, and routines. I realize now in retrospect that he really wanted a copy of himself. That he was more of a cult leader and would probably be very good friends with the likes of Charles Manson or Jim Jones if he had been in that mood and the years had been a little more accurate. At the same time, none of the gentlemen had probably had the spiritual space to share the reverence and the "truth" as they saw it.

As a participant in our small one-man cult, I became more and more irritated, frustrated, and felt terribly unworthy. "Everyone else" in our community – Carl's friends – thought that he was such a good man and so spiritually gifted and that I was probably not worthy of his "salvation". There were those who explicitly said that to me, even in front of Carl, who just agreed. In other words, their behavior only confirmed what I felt myself, so it must be true. It was devastating to have it "confirmed" that I was useless, unworthy, and stupid.

I wanted so badly to be good enough, to be accepted, but all the time Carl found new faults in what I said or did. I started to vent through code words in the emails to Andrew, who I kept in touch with. Just as I vented myself to Elin who gave advice and support as best, she could. I had started to take a liking to Andrew more and more. We wrote long emails to each other, full of words that only he and I understood the meaning of. We both knew that Carl read through the emails and we both knew that we had crossed the line of what was verbal infidelity.

CHAPTER ELEVEN

Carl and I went on our last trip together to the United States. I never thought about myself that I would cross the physical line of infidelity. I didn't understand then what my longing and thirst for belonging, closeness and love would lead to. I didn't understand that a deeply offended, angry and scorned man who had never had to answer for anything in his entire life and who had always had his way, could become a psychologically dangerous man. I didn't have that overview at the time, but I would get that insight shortly. On this trip, I was physically unfaithful to Carl, along with Andrew.

To this day, I don't know what I thought about it, really. I have repressed a lot. Partly because I felt that I was carrying out such a huge betrayal of my then husband, and partly because at the same time I lived in a constant betrayal of myself. This, constantly letting yourself down, is a function of all the dysfunctional pieces within you. All experiences, everything one has been taught about life and oneself and everything one has made up about oneself and one's inadequacy, all these are the breeding grounds for worries along the path of life and it is one's duty and responsibility to deal with it.

But what happens on a large reservation in the middle of the desert is not always completely secret. Someone had seen Andrew and me together, hand in hand, some elusive kiss, the looks. This someone told Carl who was furious. He was understandably deeply offended and upset. But it all took to extremes. His previously calmer, more passive-aggressive temperament was as if blown away immediately. I stood for what I had done, admitted everything without hesitation. Told in detail about the sexual act with Andrew to answer Carl's demanding requests. I also stood for the fact that our relationship was broken and that I didn't feel well. I was ready to move out and I would do it as soon as we got home from the US. Carl would never have to see me again. Maybe a part of me cheated to get a ticket out of an unhealthy relationship?

Contrary to what I expected, Carl absolutely did not want us to divorce. Nor that I would move out. I owed it to him to stay, he said, and I believed him. I had let him down, but he would forgive me. He claimed. And I believed him. I was deeply confused, had expected to be kicked out, expected a divorce. But that didn't happen.

On the other hand, a few years of emotional and psychological abuse and sexual abuse and torment followed. His need for control became even greater and I had to have all phone calls on speakerphone, all emails had to be read through by him an extra time, he sent several threatening letters to Andrew from my email address and forbade me to ever mention him again. It all degenerated so much that I was deeply depressed, and Carl was deeply offended and became a fulltime alcoholic. We had daily fights and conflicts. He abused me verbally, emotionally, psychologically, and sexually every day. He introduced me as "the whore" when we met someone acquaintance. No one said anything, just gave me pity looks, but no one marked that it was wrong. So even though I was hurt by what he said and did, I assumed I deserved it. I had no frames of reference, no guidelines.

My parents had violated each other and us children almost daily throughout our childhood, so for me it was already internalized as something normal in a relationship. But I was deeply unhappy within myself and together with Carl and I were unhappy for Carl's sake. I really felt that I had let him down, hurt him. After all, I had been unfaithful. He had done nothing but support me all these years. That was my thoughts.

However, Elin pointed out that what happened was not okay. That it wasn't normal and that cheating or not, you weren't allowed to hurt each other like Carl hurt me in our relationship. With her support, I managed to get Carl to agree to relationship therapy. But it didn't work. After each session, I had hope that our relationship would finally get better. But it ended up in the same rut as before. When I was twenty-five, Carl wanted to have children. I had longed for a child for years.

Elin warned me of the consequences, but at the same time was happy for me. It may seem strange that you choose to have children with someone so awful and in such a bad relationship. But I wanted and needed to be needed and wanted, I wanted and needed to mean something more than being Carl's "whore", an appendage, a pseudo-existence in someone else's life.

Everyone except Elin only knew me as Carl's wife. I was not a person of my own. I was nothing more than his wife. Carl's wife, who had also cheated on him. Failed him. I was the appendage whore that he most humbly and magnanimously had kept in his life. I began to hate that existence.

The desire for a small child to love and nurture together with self-denial about the real deal of the relationship, was the basis for what happened later. We got pregnant on the first try and Carl lit up. He offended me less but didn't stop completely. He promised healing and repentance and I believed him. He was to quit smoking and stop drinking as soon as the baby was born. I was overjoyed to be pregnant. I loved the baby long before they were born. And I was scared. So deeply afraid of losing the baby that I cried with anxiety every day. I was so afraid that they would die that I could barely breathe. But the pregnancy went on as usual, everything looked good, and the birth went well.

A healthy and cuddly little baby was born on a stormy winter's day, and I loved them deeply, a kind of love you can't explain, it must be experienced. The child and

I stayed in the hospital for two more days after the birth, I didn't want to go home. But we couldn't stay there longer than we did, we had to get home. Carl picked us up at the maternity ward and drove us home in the now fading snowstorm.

My joy at our little miracle quickly turned to anxiety and anger because as soon as we got home, Carl said that from now on our child was *my* responsibility as a woman and then he started drinking as if his previous promises and praises to stop drinking had never been spoken. I sat in our rocking chair and cried in silence while I breastfed the little one and realized there and then that nothing will ever change unless I create this change myself. Carl had just abandoned our child. He would never change his mind. Our child would grow up under the same circumstances as I did, and it was a thought I couldn't live with. I realized that I had to take responsibility, that I had put too much responsibility on Carl.

All these years I had been waiting for him to change, for him to stop behaving the way he did. Never that I had thought that I would make other demands, that I could leave the relationship. That maybe I even deserved to leave the relationship. It was completely foreign thoughts to me. With the consequences of my infidelity still in mind, I concluded that I had to keep this a secret, otherwise I would never be able to escape.

It took two years to secretly plan the move in detail together with Elin and the local priest in the village where Carl and I lived. During this time, I developed postpartum depression with an abysmal fear of losing the baby. I didn't dare to leave them, didn't dare let anyone else look after them, couldn't sleep for longer periods without waking up panicking, thinking they might be dead. I realized that this panic and anxiety was unsustainable and got help from the health care center, to get in touch with a psychologist. He was friendly, but not very attentive.

After four sessions, he considered me to be "cured" and discharged me as a patient. In my mind, everything was still chaos and the feeling of being worthless, at the mercy of others as well as being stupid, filled me to the brim.

The months went by slowly, and the feeling of constant panic and worry made me contact a psychologist again. This time it was a woman. The meeting lasted about twenty minutes.

After gently telling me about my postpartum depression and the ever-present panic and anxiety, she replied that I was too intellectual to need help and support. Her assessment was that I could rationalize myself out of my mental misery and therefore people like me could not go to psychologists. I got up and left without paying and she didn't stop me. New psychologist sessions were not even in question the next few years. I never again wanted to feel as unnecessary as I did in these short meetings with psychologists.

Then came the day when Carl was presented with divorce papers and the date of moving. He was incredibly angry and stated that he felt betrayed, cheated, and manipulated by me. I let him feel that way. He had to sign the papers and under verbal abuse and threats, the child and I moved out of the house with the help of my father and Elin. Something changed that day when I gathered up the few possessions I and my child had, what little of my dignity and brain activity I had left.

The following months my child and I lived in economic poverty but in spiritual wealth. We lived under threats and harassment from Carl who entered our home without permission, who called on my phone through the night and hissed threats in my ears. But he eventually stopped harassing us, mostly because he would be publicly humiliated if I let out the truth about him. It was my secret weapon. Stick to the rules of the game and you get to keep your job and your reputation in the city. Violate them and I will file a police report, and everyone will know who you truly are.

In the early days, I had no income other than the governmental child benefit as well as governmental housing benefits. We didn't always have food on the table or heating in the home. There were days when we went hungry and nights when we were cold. Thanks to Elin and her family, we had a roof over our heads when they paid the rent and electricity. They came over with lunch boxes, clothes, and toys whenever they had the opportunity to spare them. I am eternally grateful to her for this. My other childhood friend, Paulina, came into my life again. She gave me a personal loan to settle all the expensive debts that had accumulated over the years due to Carl's short-sightedness about money and my "prohibition" to seek more profitable jobs than hourly employment. I am also grateful to her, eternally grateful.

After four months, my dream of studying at university was fulfilled. I had applied for just about all the courses that I was eligible for, which was a lot, I had good qualifications from both high school and adult education. Knowledge has always been stimulating and fun for me. I like to read and investigate. I swore that I would accept the first school I got into and did so. This meant money, student aid and student loans and a future to get better jobs and better opportunities for my child and me.

I first took a summer course on American history and then got the news that I was accepted to the Sociology and Behavioral Sciences program at the local university. I had no idea what it was, what it would lead to or how it worked, I just took a chance.

The first summer without Carl, I once again invited a man into my and my child's life. I would later learn to be more restrained when it comes to relationships in general and intimate relationships in particular. But it would take a while. First, I needed to learn a thing or two the more irritated and painful way.

Magnus, a young man my own age, was at first friendly, polite, and nice. As in all unhealthy relationships, we quickly became a couple and moved in together, moving to a new apartment in a better, more affluent middle-class area. I liked Magnus, but I think it would be wrong to say that I loved him. After Carl, I was very unsure of what the concepts of "loving someone" really meant. I was still tarnished, mentally tender and vulnerable, and was more reserved towards others. But this suspicion and feeling of vulnerability, I hid deep inside. Never let anyone understand how I felt or what I really thought. Over the years, I had learned to keep quiet about certain things, to keep secrets. I had not yet learned to be honest with myself or to be completely honest in relationships.

The first two years with Magnus were good, except that I didn't really like his parents. They didn't really like me or my child either. They thought I was too much "white trash" for their nice little boy. They came from a more affluent family. They thought that I had a bad influence on him, because he started to tell them off when they interfered in our relationship. They thought I was strange, different, and not in a positive way. It wasn't anything they said to me or Magnus directly, not at first. But they came with small hints, comments and looks. I felt that neither I nor my child fit into their family. It was just that his parents tolerated our presence.

There is a reason why you should not be in a hurry to get a new partner after a breakup. Especially not after living in an unhealthy relationship. The risks of being blind to new violations are imminent, as is the fact that you are often unaware of your own behaviors and shortcomings in the relationships you create. But I didn't know this at the time. I didn't know what patterns of behavior I was dragging into the relationship or what behaviors he was dragging into the relationship or how these would interfere. I was unaware that I was picking up where I left off the previous relationship, with a lack of judgment and a lack of trust.

After a while, Magnus began to show tendencies to be jealous of my child. Used as he was to being the family's golden boy, the youngest son and barely even cut the umbilical cord even though he was an adult. He thought that my child was taking up too much of my time and had a very hard time understanding why I would rather spend time with my child than with him. He didn't have much understanding of their personality, which is of the sensitive and reserved kind, he didn't understand that children need closeness and love. He thought that my love for my child left him without love and could no longer distinguish between my child being a small child in need of care and motherly love and he is being a grown-ass man. So, he began to behave contemptuously and threateningly toward them. He avoided them or made nasty comments or taunts when they were around or said something.

One day he stood and yelled at them, leaning over them where they lay in the fetal position and screaming in fear. The reason for Magnus' outburst was that my child didn't want to say hello to him that day. I got angry and threw him out immediately. Attacking my child was a boundary that no one was ever allowed to cross. Never, never ever.

And that's a limit I've always stuck to. After that, it wasn't a question of whether the relationship was dead, it was an undisputed fact. Magnus did show great remorse for his action, but a line had been crossed and there was nothing else in this universe he could do but move and never speak to me nor my child ever again. This is how it had to be and so it was. Two months later, he moved out and my child and I moved to a smaller apartment where we lived in peace during my last semester at university. But I was unfortunately not done yet in my dysfunctional behavior.

CHAPTER TWELVE

Even though my child and I lived in peace from Magnus and Carl, we did not live in peace from my siblings. At this point I didn't have contact with Arnie, Amanda, or Fredric, but decent contact with Oliver, Jasmine, and Sandra. Things had been cracking at the seams lately where our parents, who had gone their separate ways under very aggressive forms, slandered each other in front of me and my siblings. We were still expected to take a stand between the two.

Anyone who took the "wrong" side, became an object of hatred for a long time to come. Not only by the parents, but also by the siblings who "belonged" to one of the parents. There were insults over text messages and phone calls about how useless, disgusting, and stupid you were. Despite this, I volunteered to help with this and that, hoping and believing that this time it will be different, only to be betrayed and disappointed again.

Amanda, Arnie, and Fredric had moved with our mother to an apartment, while Sandra and Oliver lived with our father. Jasmine lived in her own apartment. It was very difficult to keep any balance between all the feuds that were going on. However, Amanda unexpectedly contacted me one day, and wondered if I could help her with her education. She studied to be an assistant nurse at Komvux. In my previously mentioned eagerness to be of help and support, I said yes, of course! I understand today that I unconsciously tried to make up for all the "mistakes" I had made, such as that I was placed in a foster home and not them, that I had good grades and continued studying at university and not them, simply that I had moved on in life in a, for them, different way.

Anyway, we suddenly had close contact, me and my child went home to Amanda several times a week. I basically wrote all her homework assignments, home exams and essays. It was wrong of me to cheat but blinded by a bad conscience for my aforementioned move and by Amanda's pleas for help, I allowed myself to agree. At every meeting, Amanda complained about how her partner treated her badly. She told me that he was jealous and violent. I gave her lots of information about support lines and what help she could get from the Police and Social Services. I was happy to be able to help her get away from a destructive relationship and get an education so that she could get a job and provide for her child who was then around a year old. I thought in my stupidity that we had a good contact and would continue to have it that way.

Then came the day when she had her last home exam and was to get her final grade. She passed the class with a C, and I was very happy for her. We had decided before that day, that I would visit the day after the graduation. So, I got on the bus to get to her. In the meantime, I called her up to ask if we should meet below her apartment and go for a walk or if we should sit with her. I didn't get an answer. I texted and called several times. Still got no answer. I started to get a bad feeling in my body, so I called her again, this time with a hidden number. She answered and sounded annoyed that it was me. I asked why she didn't answer when I called before. Her answer still amazes me today: she replied that she had dropped her mobile phone on the floor and therefore some calls did not arrive... It sounded too pathetic to be true, so I wondered again how it came about that a hidden number got through and not a visible number. She replied stressed that she didn't know, but that unfortunately we won't meet that day, maybe another day? She needed to leave her mobile phone to a repairman.... I said, okay, and we decided on a new day and time.

That day and time came and went, and she continued not to answer my calls or texts. When I called again from a hidden number, she answered. This time it was said that after the repair, some numbers had tragically disappeared from her mobile, and my number was among the "lost" numbers. I didn't want to believe that she was really ghosting me and trying to prevent all possible opportunities to meet, so I tried to get hold of her for a few weeks. Eventually, I realized that she had only used me to achieve her goal: an education. After that, she discarded me like a garbage bag. I meant nothing more to her than a means to get where she wanted. She had manipulated me to reach her goal and had no plans whatsoever to have any future relationship with me. I had been stupid and blind to the signals. I stopped contacting her.

At the same time, Sandra and Jasmine began to behave strangely. They were evasive and occasionally wrote hateful text messages to me and I didn't understand why. In the end, Sandra said that she and Jasmine had planned to stab my child at the next time we met. Partly to get revenge for moving away from home as a teenager, partly because Amanda had spread rumors that I had allegedly reported her to the Social Services for child abuse, and partly because I had allegedly tried to spy on her through said Social Services. I didn't understand anything. It was so unreal and strange that I questioned their mental health. Neither Sandra nor Jasmine, or even for that matter, Oliver, believed me when I explained that I have nothing to do with any social services report. Had it been from me, I would have had no problem writing my name because I have no problem standing up for children's rights.And the whole" spy thing" was just morbid.

I said they need help, and I can't give them that help. I also filed a police report for unlawful threats, which unfortunately was dropped due to lack of evidence. I had no hopes of any prosecution or a verdict, but if something were to happen, I wanted the Police to know who they were going to look for. It all sounds distorted and absurd, but unfortunately that's how my siblings have developed. They took all the sick parts from our upbringing with them and embraced them, where I did what I could to break these behaviors. Unfortunately, this created an abysmal gap between us and me and my child became more and more socially isolated from the family. For many years, I thought about what I was doing wrong, why it was so easy for Amanda to just use me like that and then spread rumors and slander to our siblings, relatives, and others.

It was only in recent years that I have come to understand that this kind of behavior arises in people who need to dominate and control their surroundings and who have a pathological jealousy. As soon as a person starts to be perceived as a threat to their self-image, need for dominance and has something that the person in question is jealous of, they start spreading rumors and shattering all social ties that exist between them and the person who is being victimized. The purpose of this behavior is to make the person who is the victim of rumor spread more vulnerable to future attacks. It is simply a way of ensuring that the truth never comes out, and if it does, then no one believes it. There is a kind of moral disconnection that justifies harmful behavior, that justifies rumors and social division.

I now realize that since I was the one who actually did all the elements of the assistant nurse education, except for showing up at the mandatory meetings, I was sitting on information that would shake the image Amanda wanted to have in others. My existence in her life or even close social life (siblings and relatives), meant that I could at any time reveal that she had cheated her way through the education. I could also tell others around her about the alleged violence in the relationship, which I suspect wasn't true either. In other words, she wanted to protect her social status, which was based on dishonesty and her abuse and manipulation of other people. The fact that most of my siblings, our parents and relatives followed and still follow the same pattern, I have understood is that in such group dynamics as our family constellation are, it creates a positive feedback loop of escalating violence. In this case, psychological, social, and emotional violence.

I was also part of this loop before. But I took the opportunity to break out of it. I was given the opportunity for another life, outside the family, that my siblings did not get. I also believe that this has contributed greatly to my siblings' hatred, anger, and bitterness. Which would later turn out to lead to a cruel revenge. Escalating hostility towards a person usually has its roots in unprocessed trauma, jealousy, and bitterness. My siblings all carry unprocessed traumas. I carried and still carry unprocessed traumas. In my eyes, I don't understand what she and other siblings are so jealous of really; Even though I have been working hard on getting out of our dysfunctional learned behaviors during the time, I was still practicing a lot of these behaviors at this point. I didn't feel good mentally or emotionally, I had difficulty forming good, sustainable relationships and lacked community. I was groomed by an older man and tricked into a dysfunctional and unhealthy relationship. I self-harmed, had suicidal thoughts and considered myself a very worthless individual who didn't deserve anything. It's nothing to be jealous of.

CHAPTER THIRTEEN

Alongside my studies, I had started working. I had a permanent part-time job and suffered severely from both anxiety and the aforementioned imposter syndrome. Since I was studying at university, I contacted the university's student health team, because I felt that I needed to talk to someone. Again. The anxiety and probably a deep depression was so severe that I had difficulty managing my daily life. Of course, I took care of the child, the home, the job, and the studies, but felt less and less joy. Mostly I was just empty and felt meaningless, as if I was sitting in a glass jar and could only look at life, but not participate on an emotional level.

I was a little over thirty years old, a single, autistic parent of an autistic special-needs child. The relationship with my parents and siblings was almost non-existent. I thus encountered the university's student health service, which had an older man, a priest, who acted as a kind of counsellor. Gunnar was different and seemed friendly and caring.

I felt that he cared about me and how I felt. I dared to tell a little about how I felt, how I had it emotionally and what I had been through in my previous relationships. I felt a support and again a hope that maybe I could belong.

There was a big gap between my adult self and the little abused and neglected child who was also me and I couldn't tell them apart. The little child remembered all the painful events, all the bad words, all the insults. My adult self, claimed that it no longer mattered, I was an adult now. We all have behaviors, perceptions, thoughts, and feelings that are inherited within the family. These behaviors, perceptions, thoughts, and feelings become habits, and habits are difficult to break.

When it comes to behavioral and emotional patterns that we inherit through the family we grow up in, we usually choose to keep these even if they are not healthy for us. We can choose to put an end to them, by actively making choices that lead us away from destructive actions, patterns, and behaviors. But we can only make these choices when we become aware of our own participation and responsibility. That life does not "happen to us" but that we are involved in creating the life that we have, with all that it entails. In the meantime, we'll behave in an unhealthy way, make harmful decisions, and commit actions that go against what we really want to achieve in life. You become your own enemy. Before I found this out, I was living my life according to the behaviors I knew. So, I sought affirmation, belonging and community and thirsted to be loved and seen by someone, anyone. Even by another self-righteous, narcissistic old man.

Gunnar, like Carl before him, made me his personal project. He was twenty-two years older than me and gave me gifts and compliments that I received suspiciously He invited me to lunches and gave me the confirmation and belonging I still sought and longed for. I was admittedly more cautious than before, I never fully trusted Gunnar and was open about the fact that I didn't have much trust. Previous relationships had left their mark.

Despite his profession, Gunnar chose to try to disprove my lack of trust by spending more and more time with me. Give more and more attention, compliments, gifts, thoughtful texts, and calls. He brought Christmas presents for me and my child when it was Christmas, brought gifts on our birthdays, surprised with flowers and presents in between, and swore that he would never even think about bringing back gifts.

I began to rely more and more on him because he constantly wanted to prove that he was not "like the others". He wanted to prove that he was different. There were times when I wanted to interrupt what was emerging, but I didn't. I wanted to believe that he was different, that I was finally, really accepted, loved, and belonged. I was open about the fact that even though I felt loving feelings for him, I didn't want an intimate relationship.

That maturity had grown throughout the years, and it felt important for me to live in intimate abstinence. I was never sexually or romantically interested in Gunnar, he was not attractive in my eyes, but he offered security and stability. That's also what he claimed and that's what I chose to believe. For someone who had always lacked security and stability, it was like being offered stars, gold and diamonds, a castle, and a unicorn at the same time. It was extremely tempting and very difficult to resist. As a person, I liked him a lot, he really wanted to "prove" what a good man he was and that I and my child were safe with him.

When we talked about our so-called relationship, I was open about the fact that I wanted a *genuine* relationship, with *genuine, unconditional* love, belonging and community. Not the kind of nonsense you saw in movies or read about in short stories. Certainly not a relationship built on sex, demands or other conditions than showing each other respect. He agreed with all this. At least that's what he claimed. He talked far and wide about us being "soul mates", so perfectly created for each other, like yin and yang, despite the age difference. He explained that he was a little older and did not want to live alone for the rest of his time and me and the child could live in a big house out in the countryside. It was a winning concept for all parties, according to his logic. We all got community, security, and stability. That sounded good, didn't it?

Somewhere inside me something was chafing but I didn't know what it was or how to listen to that very, very weak, pecking little voice. But at least I knew that we were not soul mates. That much I knew.

Diary entry September 1, 2019:

"We don't have a traditional relationship. He is kind of old and I chose to accept his offer of cohabitation to secure for my child's wellbeing. Alone we are very much at each other's mercy and if something happened to me, they would have no one to turn to."

Gunnar often talked about how we were going to live together, me and my child and himself and his two adult children, Lisa, and Loki. We were all supposed to live free from pressure, stress, and unreasonable demands. The artistic sides of both me and my child would blossom, and I would have a huge garden to work in. Something I appreciated a lot; I have always liked gardening.

At the beginning of any relationship, no matter how it's formed, it usually sounds good. It may also sound great. You want to believe that it is something good. It's like being blind in one eye and having a severe visual defect in the other. And have neither glasses nor lenses. Although it *sounded* good, the relationship was not completely frictionless. Surprise, surprise…Gunnar was married but was in the process of divorce as he said.

He showed me the divorce papers that he was waiting for her to sign, but which she refused to do. Just like with Carl, the woman Gunnar was married to was claimed to be crazy, egocentric, and difficult to "get rid of". According to Gunnar's statement, he could not "just throw her out" and she "refused to move". This should have been a very clear signal for me to let it all go and move on. Of course, I didn't.

There was a lot I hadn't learned in life. I had never learned about healthy relationships or about boundaries other than "violate my child and it's over". However, I had learned to avoid and ignore my feelings and dismiss what I saw, unless it concerned my child. I kept an eye on my child and did not leave them alone for a long time with anyone, especially not a man, just in case the man in question should have a sudden bout of jealousy and attack them. Despite my "blindness", I was both annoyed and frustrated by Gunnar's claim about the "insane wife" and pointed out that what he said and what he did, seem to be two completely different things. That he whined about the fact that this ex-wife lived in his home, but he didn't seem to make any demands on her to actually move out. A bit like he wasn't completely honest with me about the relationship.

However, Gunnar was eloquent and skilled at diverting and manipulating. He had explanations and excuses for everything and continued to paint a fantasy picture of the two of us and my child, living in his large villa. There, my child and I could be just as creative and free as we wanted and needed to be. We would have better finances, a large garden and lots of fun activities to do. All that was better than the small, limited, and expensive two-room apartment we lived in with neighbors who bothered and complained almost every week? If I just had a little patience with his "crazy and fragile" ex-wife, everything would be fine. He really couldn't *make a scene* in front of his children? *Did I demand* that of him, perhaps? To cause his children the spiritual pain that would come from their parents divorcing? Wasn't it *enough for him to get divorced and promise me and my child security and stability? Could I not then allow* him to sort out his divorce as gently as possible with their poor children? I thought he was a bit overly protective of his children, after all, they were both over twenty years old. They were adults. But his reasoning and the fact that he triggered my already existing feelings of guilt about everything in life and that he knew very well that I had, made it difficult for me to come up with counterarguments without feeling even stupider and very mean and selfish.

Now in retrospect, I understand that Gunnar, like Carl and Magnus, played the guilt game, just like my parents and siblings did, and that I went for it. I fell for the well-known behavior and took the blame for being nagging, selfish and demanding, albeit more reluctantly than before. I had started to wake up to an understanding of my behaviors, not thanks to Gunnar, but thanks to other sources such as Iyanla Vanzant, Dr.

Phil and Martha Beck. All three, whose books and podcasts I had started listening to more diligently, brought up this with choosing similar relationships until the day you realize what you have done and created in your life. I began to realize that I had been attracting and *attracted to* all these critical, deranged and degrading men who liked to play the guilt game, because I needed to learn to recognize it in order to then break free from it. Unfortunately, some progress is slow, so it took a while before I really saw Gunnar for who he was and what he really stood for.

CHAPTER FOURTEEN

Eventually, Gunnar's ex-wife moved out with the divorce papers in hand and me and my child moved in. With deep anxiety for me. Had I really done the right thing? In retrospect, I realize that I should have listened to my gut feeling that this wasn't such a great idea. But as mentioned before, I didn't have much experience listening to myself. I had only just begun to actively reflect on my life, my experiences, my relationships with others and my behavior, what I brought into the relationships and what others brought with them. As soon as we had moved in, I mean already on the second day, difficult conflicts arose.

Gunnar was very keen that everything in his house should be as he decided. I wasn't allowed to unpack most of my things or put my things anywhere I liked. There were strictly designated places, which I graciously allowed to put a few of my things. He inspected every single gadget and decided if it fit in or not. He didn't think most of it fit in and therefore wasn't allowed to be there.

But this time I didn't let myself be bullied like before, so I made demands. I demanded that I would be allowed to make my mark in the home, if it would be "our" home, which was what he had promised all the time we didn't live together. This, of course, led to more conflicts, because Gunnar always used his "My wife *always* ignored me and made decisions over my head! Now you do it too!" Again, he played diligently on my feelings of guilt and shame by comparing me to "his wife" as he always called her, despite the divorce, and how horrible she was. Then I was also horrible and ungrateful. I was *just* like her....

Most reluctantly, I kept quiet in many, many situations so as not to create more conflicts. But sometimes they were unavoidable. Gunnar wanted the home as it had always been, and I was not allowed to change anything. I wasn't allowed to put up a painting, or even hit a nail without checking with him first if it was okay. If I didn't do this, he would throw us out on the streets. In order not to become homeless right away, I partly did as he said. But it came at a cost. Every day, I thought about what to do: adapt or find a new home for me and the child? Maybe it was me who was wrong, maybe I was the one who was too selfish and demanding as others had also claimed? Was it harmful for my child and me to stay in this house? There was no physical violence, and the conflicts took place when the child was not at home. What did I really know about relationships? Maybe Gunnar was right, that with time it would get better?

Diary entry June 12, 2020:

"Gunnar always comments about my clothes and my appearance. I don't like it here at all and haven't done so since we moved in. It's his house, his interior. His, his, his! Where do we fit? He thinks that we take up too much space, that we - me and my beloved child, take up too much space! We share a bedroom, a wardrobe, and a desk in one room! Is that to take up too much space? There are five rooms left! Something is really wrong with him..."

However, the anger and frustration from years of oppression and violations bubbled under the surface and my way of dealing with it was by withdrawing from Gunnar more and more. To stay away both physically and mentally.

Despite his professional role as a priest and counselor, despite his knowledge that he said he had, and even though I had explicitly spoken out, Gunnar felt that my withdrawal was not a symptom of feeling depressed, that I was stressed about having ended up in and created yet another dysfunctional relationship, that I was dysregulated and had difficulty finding balance in life. He, just like Carl, saw me rather as a problem that had to be corrected, adapted to his wishes and his needs. I didn't fit into his perception of how the world and especially women should behave, I didn't fit into the fantasy he had created about us and therefore it was me who was wrong.

I tried to force myself to be close to Gunnar and tried to force myself to be content and happy. But I wasn't, and it didn't go well at all to force social situations. Much of the time was simply spent avoiding Gunnar, Lisa and

Loke. I avoided eating with them, eating with my child in another room or at a later time. I only spent time with my child to avoid having to spend time with anyone else in the household and I made sure that my child didn't spend much time with them either.

You might think that you should "show up" at holidays like Christmas, New Year, Midsummer, etc., but I couldn't stand the anxiety and pain it meant to sit there and listen to their loud talk, their smacking and their critical looks and sneering smiles at me and my child. Above all, I didn't want to expose my child to the social shitstorm it meant to be social with Gunnar, Loke and Lisa, so I made sure we stayed away. Gunnar, Lisa and Loke were so fake that it disgusted me. My stupidity of having fallen into the trap, *again*, disgusted me. I was so incredibly angry at myself for making such an incredibly foolhardy decision.

Gunnar became increasingly frustrated and offended and showed it by commenting on me and my child and our appearances and bodies. He was criticizing that we did not spend time with him, Loke and Lisa and their partners. He couldn't understand why I or my child never wanted to spend time with them. In his world, it was specifically me who was wrong, and he demanded that I talk to a psychologist, or he would kick me and my child out. Make us homeless. One might ask what kind of man, a priest on top of that, threatens homelessness when he doesn't get what he wants? A disgusting person, I would say. A cowardly, selfish scumbag.

On the other hand, why didn't we just move out again? During this period, I was still not fully aware of what was happening inside me or around me. I was busy dealing with my past in the only way I could- by forcing myself to do other things. I was busy being a parent of a child with special needs and dealing with the evenly strained, disgustingly false association with Gunnar and his disgusting children. In addition to this, I tried to manage my work, where I felt inadequate, unnecessary, incompetent, and worthless.

During this time, I was simply so busy with everything around me and I was so strongly socialized in that I am the root of all faults and mistakes in all relationships and I am the one who must change. So, I tried that too, which I failed to do, because it was not in my true nature to be "like everyone else" or "do like everyone else". I considered moving, several times. I didn't feel at home or even welcome. But I wanted to give Gunnar a chance, he was very convincing about the coming "perfect life", and he often insisted that I needed to show my child what "good relationships looked like" so that we were not as alone and left out as we had been before. He was right, we were very lonely, isolated and at each other's mercy before and it would be good for them to experience good relationships.

So, at Gunnar's request, I extremely reluctantly contacted a psychologist once again. Gunnar's idea about the psychologist contact was to "come to terms with the fact that I wasn't docile enough", that I refused to eat at the same table as him and that I refused to have sex with him, despite that I had been very clear about not wanting an intimate relationship. The fact that all this was my essential self, which Beck talks about in her books, trying to protect me and my child from a harmful relationship, was not something that was on the map at the time. But in retrospect, I understand that this reluctance and avoidance to be close to these people stemmed from the fact that we were not good for each other and our inner, essential selves, told us so by making it as uncomfortable as possible for each of us.

Despite Gunnar's conviction of "our future good life together", I wasn't good for him either. Otherwise, he wouldn't have had to try to force a relationship in the first place. I have understood it to be that a good relationship flows more naturally, not spasmodic and forced. I didn't live in the relationship the way Gunnar wanted me to, and with the help of the psychologist I would, according to Gunnar, be "corrected" so I did all those things that were important to Gunnar. So that his fantasy could become reality without me putting a spanner in the works and stop working against his dream life. Very clear signs that we were not good for each other...

Anyway, I was strongly against contacting another psychologist, with the other failed sessions in good memory, as well as how things went between me and Gunnar. But for my child's sake, I did, because I thought that if I manage to adapt to Gunnar so that it becomes a good relationship, my child will see a

healthy relationship when they grow up and we don't

have to be so alone. And we get to belong and be

involved.

Martin, a young psychologist surprised me. In addition to being intelligent for real and not pseudo-intelligent like Gunnar, Carl, or Magnus, he was also well-read and very wise. Almost a little too wise for his age. At first, I was extremely skeptical, expecting him to shrug his shoulders and say that it didn't work. That my problems were not "real" problems. I was terribly afraid of being dismissed, abandoned, and left to my own devices, like so many other times before.

But Martin helped me understand that Gunnar was claiming parts of me that I was unconsciously not willing to hand over. He realized that my issues with Gunnar lay deeper within me and had their origins somewhere else entirely. That I had brought some dysfunctional behaviors into the relationship, just as Gunnar was guaranteed to have dysfunctional behaviors as well. But since it was me, Martin talked to and not Gunnar, it was me he had to work with.

Which he did by working on these parts through something called exposure therapy. It was incredibly hard, demanding, and painful to rummage through all the memories, feelings, and abuse. I hated the exercises I had to do, but it was time to change things now. Martin helped me to set boundaries, to listen more to myself and to dare to break the spiral of anxiety, worry, depressive thoughts and self-harming behaviors (entering dysfunctional relationships is a kind of self-harming behavior). In the meantime, I really tried to do my utmost to create a good relationship with Gunnar, because somewhere I thought that it might be possible to live up to at least parts of his fantasy of the "fantastic family". The sex would not be on the map. It was a demand I would never agree to. It was impossible to even imagine. Unfortunately, Gunnar lacked the ability to see others and see change as something positive.

After a lot of ifs and buts, tons of nagging, I managed to be allowed to repaint the kitchen. It was not with joy or curiosity that Gunnar agreed to this, and it was not with joy or positivity that it ended with. It ended in Gunnar, after still a lot of criticism and insults about my way of painting, doing everything himself again. To show me how to "do the job for real" while he pointed out that I had destroyed his home. I wanted to drown him in the paint can but refrained. While he said that I was actively destroying his home with my ideas and basically mere presence, Gunnar also pointed out that I should feel at home, which was very confusing to me. I never figured out how he wanted me to be, because no matter what I did, it was wrong, and I "ruined" something.

He became completely hysterical when I on my own initiative repaired two cupboard doors that could not be closed. He meant that I should have asked first how to fix doors so he could show me, how to fix "the right way". I was deeply offended by this, because I had shown that I could fix the cabinet myself and I had also been denouncing the broken cabinet for several months. But he firmly denied this, it was just something I had made up. We had never talked about it before, but he just came home from work and then I had destroyed his home, again.

I became more and more clear that the state of his mental health was messed up, and I became more and more doubtful about whether I should really try to adapt to his conditions. He was obviously a self-righteous *mansplainer*, i.e. a man who thinks he knows better than women just because he is a man and therefore has to explain how things work, especially to women, who are considered uneducated and stupid.

The mansplainer Gunnar's condition was that I would be with him as a wife. He wanted to get married and have *his* dream wedding. I wanted to wait, because I didn't think the relationship was really going in the right direction. He wasn't interested in hearing how I wanted it but expected me to drink all his words like nectar. It became disgusting in the end. He wanted big parties with a lot of people and thought I was dull and boring who didn't want parties at all and definitely not many people around me.

He meant that I should just "adapt" like "good people do". In other words, he wronged me, my experiences, my way of functioning and my personality, time and time again. He put me in the group of "evil or defective" people. But this time, the mental and emotional chafing became more tender and thus more tangible. My dislike of Gunnar, Loke and Lisa grew every day, every week and every month. Thankfully, nothing lasts forever. My neglect of myself did not last forever either.

One day Gunnar complained again about my desire to rearrange the living room (everything in the home looked the same as it had for twenty years and it was really depressing to be in) and said "I'd rather burn the whole house, than have you put your hands on it. It's *my* house and *I decide* how it should look! You just come here and ruin everything *all the time*!". It was very good that he said that because I finally realized that he was crazy.

With a firm calmness I told him, that it was good that he said that. Then he will get what he wants. If he had received psychological support, he would probably have been diagnosed with a narcissistic personality disorder with grandiose and psychopathic traits. I realized at that moment that he had never intended to let me, and my child be ourselves. His intention had always been to control and manipulate. He only wanted me as an object that he could control, not a free individual. Although he often expressed that he liked "strong women", he never meant it. He was and is terrified of strong women. He never wanted an independent, free-thinking woman. He wanted a doll to play with, one that could live in his house and take care of him without making any claims to anything. He was a manschauvinist, in short.

Once again, I was relegated to an appendage, a pretend existence in someone else's life. On several occasions before this, not really a surprising revelation, Gunnar had complained about me and my child to Lisa and Loke and their partners, when he thought I didn't hear them. They often laughed at us behind our backs, and I just as often heard them talking about how my child and I should "learn better".

So now with a better perspective on life, I thought that, sure, I can definitely learn better and do better. By setting a limit.

Enough was enough. I had, with the help of Martin, concluded that I deserved better. My child definitely deserved better. They shouldn't have to put up with idiotic people just because their mother was an idiot too. Time for the idiot to grow up and make a series of better decisions.

CHAPTER SIXTEEN

In the midst of all this human madness where I lived out my dysfunctional behaviors, I managed to change my life and my child's life for the better. For a long time, things changed inside me. It wasn't a grand awakening à la Hollywood movies, but rather small annoying glimpses of what kind of life I had created and how the hell I had ended up there.

Through Gunnar's wishes to "correct me" and his constant criticism and verbal abuse, I did just that; I sought help so that I could make better decisions and become a better person. Obviously not in the way that Gunnar wanted and had hoped for. Something much, much better than that.One decision was to move away from Gunnar. As soon as possible. Yesterday preferably.

The second was to actively seek out more friends, so that the child and I had a social network to turn to and hang out with. A social network that consisted of people, like Elin, who like and accept us just as we are. With all our uncertainties and quirks.

During this time, despite everything that had taken place in my and Gunnar's relationship, despite everything I had processed and still needed to process, despite my exclusion from my family and relatives, I felt for the first time that I as a person mattered to myself. Not as someone's partner, someone's child, someone's friend or someone's colleague, but as just being me. It was time to gather a large amount of dignity, a good portion of responsibility, and a patience that would make Jesus seem impatient.

As time passed while waiting for a place to live, I came to realize how I had contributed to sabotaging the relationship by once again listening too much to other people's seductive talk about the "Promised Land Relationship." I had let myself be swept up in the strong normative pressure to "Be Someone's Partner", to have a car and a house, and go on a caravan vacations (I hate caravan vacations!), barbecue in the garden and play Happy Bonus Family, even if you are deeply unhappy. Other people's fantasies and ideas about what a "happy family" is, had been allowed to crowd out my own fantasies and ideas about happiness, love and the classic, The meaning of life. I lived with Gunnar's fantasy of all this, while my inner self almost clawed my eyes out in frustration. No wonder then that it was the way it was.

Gunnar, who often expressed that he "always got what he wanted", said straight out that it was his imagination, his values and his skewed perception of relationships that was the norm in that household. I was the one who didn't want to hear that side, because I wanted to belong, I wanted to be loved and accepted, I wanted social security for my child, so I let myself be persuaded by his sleazy talk about freedom, creativity and belonging. I was the one who put the lid on everything that tried to make me realize this, all the little gnawing doubts, the growing frustration, the irritation, the insomnia, the avalanche-like stress.

All these were signals that I was going against my integrity and what was good for me. It was I who really believed that Gunnar would change his mind, just like with Carl, and that if I just did "everything right" it would be fine in the end. I could just as easily have posted a Tinder Profile about "Manipulative

Psychopaths/Narcissists Wanted!". But thankfully, I didn't live very long in that denial.

This time it was different, and the change was faster than before. Previously, other people's mental problems had been interpreted as just *my* mental problems. Throughout my childhood and in all relationships, I had considered myself to be the problem, I was the one who should be "corrected", I was the one who was broken, wrong and stupid. Now other frames of reference had appeared in my mind. If the price of belonging, being loved, and having community was to give up my boundaries, my personality, my dreams, my goals, my integrity, then that was far too high a price to pay. It would give my child the wrong kind of values and principles to live by, and it was far too high a price to pay that too.

These new frames of reference also said that these broken relationships were not solely my fault, they were not just due to me. They were also due to the brokenness of the person I was in a relationship with. And that we both had a responsibility. My responsibility was first and foremost to make sure that my child was safe and grew up in a good environment. Gunnar's home was not such a place.

He was certainly not violent, but he was abusive and condescending and I could no longer accept that. Neither to be exposed to it nor that my child grew up with such a view of women. I packed up the things that belonged to me and my child and told Gunnar that we would move out as soon as we got an apartment. He got annoyed and angry but accepted that I wanted to move out. I imagine that it would give him some peace too, not having to guard *his* things and *his* home as much as he felt he needed to.

The month that followed was very stressful. I kept a good face in front of my child, wanted to show them that the best thing is to keep quiet sometimes and do your best. I stuck exclusively to them in this world of insecure adults. Gunnar was on me every day and asked what apartments I had applied for and when were we going to move. He often and gladly expressed that he longed to get rid of me, as if I were a parasite even though I paid rent and paid half of the food costs. He became more and more abusive, degrading and condescending, I no longer listened to him. I didn't even try to correct him or resist him, but just let him say what he wanted to say and then shrug his shoulders and walk away. One of the things I had learned was that people who behave the way Gunnar did and apparently do in relationships, are about power and control. If you react to the behavior, you show that there are the right buttons to push, so to speak. It gives the executive partner power and control over the recipient in the relationship. But by not reacting, I didn't give any signals that it had any effect on me, even if it was annoying and hurtful. This created frustration, as it does in those who want power but do not get what he or she wants. Thus, they find new ways to take power.

For example, Gunnar started threatening that we would not be allowed to use *his* cars, or sit on *his* chairs in the kitchen, eat *his* food in the fridge (my child and I got a shelf in the fridge for our food) among other things. "You do as I tell you or you can't drive my cars!" was one of his favorite expressions. We lived out in the country and needed the cars; he knew very well that he would make a mess of it for us if we couldn't use the cars. Which I told him. With a sneering smile he said, "give me the keys or do as I say". He got the car keys. Which he gave back after a couple of days when he realized that he, Loke or Lisa in that case had to drive my child to and from school on the following weekdays. It was not something they were interested in. Instead, I was required to refuel the car just as much as I had driven it, which I did. He would check the odometer reading and calculate the exact cost (I zeroed it after every drive out of sheer spite), which made him frustrated, but he didn't want to drive every morning, so he mostly ranted.

I would also tell him exactly where I was going and how long I would be there and I would always ask for permission every time I would use the car, even if he knew I was only going to school and work. He had to be kept with his violations and attempts to control our lives, I didn't really care what he said anymore because secretly I had already signed a first-hand contract for an apartment on the other side of the town, we live in. I took care of both the search, the viewing and the contract writing between pick-up at school and home. I didn't mention anything about the apartment to him, nothing about the moving date or anything else. I took care of everything in the greatest secrecy, with the help of Elin and the newfound friends Angelika, Philip, Ariola and Jasko. It's strange that, how life crises create opportunities and open new paths that you didn't see before.

The fact that I have chosen to keep things secret on both occasions, when it has concerned men with an unhealthy need for control, is because of their need for control. People who demand transparency in everything that concerns one's life, are people who need strict boundaries between "mine" and "theirs" and it is also a person you should never give too much information to. Such a person would most often try to manipulate, sabotage, and persuade in order to maintain control, and you cannot afford that from an emotional and psychological perspective.

I've never been interested in going back to the same person if I've left them once or if I'm in the process of breaking free from such a relationship. I have believed in what is called "love" by people, but it has only been disguised self-loathing and self-denial. By becoming more and more aware of my own behavior in a relationship and in relation to the other person, I have learned to keep my cards to myself, develop myself and go where I need to go, no matter how painful and humiliating it has been.

Some acquaintances have occasionally expressed derisively that I would "like" old men, since both Carl and Gunnar are significantly older than I am. These people certainly do not have the whole background and they are especially not aware of the processes behind childhood trauma and how these affect one's choices in life if one does not become aware of them. But no matter what, it's painful to be mocked for the relationships you create. That others openly laugh at you when they hear about the age differences that have been and come with comments, it's not funny and I get sad when people do that. These are not bad or stupid people, but ignorant and superficial. They never look in depth and they forget that there is a person behind those relationships, a person who has different reasons why they have made bad decisions.

Again, not as excuses, simply just the fact that there are always reasons behind a person's actions. That also applies to Carl, Magnus, Gunnar, and all other people. They are also teachers, these laughing people, even those who exercise violence, control, and manipulation. Through their behaviors, they make you aware of your own problem areas, such as the lack of setting healthy boundaries or the difficulty of speaking up and the thoughts and feelings that pop into your head when someone laughs at you. Like you want to punch them in the face, insult them or say something mean in return.

Likewise, what happens inside you when you are treated in an undignified and offensive way. It is the work of teachers and their behaviors and one's own actions, feelings, thoughts, and behaviors are life lessons designed to learn more about oneself and one's relationship to other people and the world around them.

Gunnar got the news of our move the same morning we moved out. I had asked to borrow the car the next day on the pretext that we were going to my child's friend's. My child knew about it all, but they were so deeply tired of living with Gunnar, Lisa, and Loke that they gladly didn't say a word about it to any of them. I had explained that it was important that we didn't say anything because then they might behave even worse. We needed to maintain the status quo and be the ones with more information than the others in the household we were leaving.

During the night while my child and everyone else slept, I packed the car as much as I could and slept only three hours. At five o'clock in the morning we left with the first moving load, without anyone waking up from it. At seven o'clock we were back at the house we moved (fled?) from and loaded more into the car. Philip was supposed to arrive with a trailer and a car at 10 am. When I stepped into the house for moving load number two, Gunnar was eating breakfast and looked generally surprised. I told him that we were moving out and that the trailer and carrying help will arrive at 10 am, so if he were a nice boy, he would let me, and my child move out without hindrance. I was honestly happy about the anxiety our sudden exit triggered in him. It was a real joy to see him snatched out of his mental cocoon, his safe zone where he had all the control and knew everything about everyone in the household and who was where.

When the color of his face had gone from chalky white to bright red, Gunnar shut himself in the living room and stayed there most of the time, just coming out to check that I wasn't taking anything that was "his". The fact that he hadn't been notified in advance made him really stressed and angry. He had wanted more control and felt betrayed and cheated, as he told Philip, when he arrived on time. I let him think so, very maliciously, too. I knew that he had wanted more control, more power, that was exactly why I didn't let him get any information whatsoever. It may seem mean, and it was definitely revenge, and even though revenge is a simple and primitive means, it was worth it.

It felt right then and still feels right today, almost four years later. You can think what you want about my actions, and usually I don't advocate revenge, but sometimes it's justified. My child and I moved into a cozy little two-room apartment and that has felt like home since we looked at it. It's wonderful! To this day, I am deeply grateful for the sanctuary that our home is for us. Just my child and me. A home where we can really be ourselves, do what we want, be as creative as we want, celebrate what we want and eat at a dining table – if we want, relaxed and unforced.

For some time, I still had the support of Martin from time to time, but it became more and more rare that I needed his guidance. For once, I have had a psychologist who has actually listened, who has understood that my anxiety and worry were due to something. It wasn't just "the way I was" or that I would be defective in some way. He didn't see me as an object, nor has he ever made any advances, no "heroic behavior" and no dismissals. He understood early on that somewhere along the course of my life I had been traumatized and through that I had learned a dysfunctional behavior. He respected me for who I was in every given moment and taught me to respect myself and for that I am eternally grateful to him.

CHAPTER SEVENTEEN

My child's and my new life in our new home was and is filled with joy and love. But the nights of the first month were filled with vivid dreams that didn't feel like dreams. In these dreams, I met my father who was crying and sad and said, *"It's too late" It's too damn late!"* and I tried to comfort him by saying, *"It's never too late. I'm here now and I love you!".* In all these dreams, which were three or four in total, my father returned and was so sincerely sad that I felt it in all my soul, even when I woke up. In the dreams, I gave him a warm hug, and both he and I cried, and he kept saying, *"It's too late! I love you, but it's too late now!"* I waited every day that I would get a call from him or from someone, I called the one sister I was in touch with, Sandra, and asked if everything was okay with everyone, she said yes. But after New Year, everything changed.

Before we get into what changed, I need to take it from the beginning for you to understand how it turned out the way it did. We must go back about two years in time before the move to the new apartment: My father had at one point, when I as a university student went to talk to Gunnar, asked why I had actually divorced Carl, he thought it would have been better if I had stayed married to him. I hadn't told my parents everything, for fear of being mocked and laughed at for my failed marriage. Not because they were any relationship-gurus, but simply that was how they handled difficult situations in our family. But this time I chose to tell it like it was, how Carl had treated me, what he had actually done during our marriage and that I didn't feel well. My dad didn't believe me. Instead, he became angry and upset, not at Carl, but at me.

He said he would talk to Carl about this because they were now friends. My father wanted to hear the truth from him instead, and I felt the world disappear under my feet. I had somehow distorted thought that at least my father would listen to me, that he, if anyone, would give me support because he was the one, I had the best contact with during all the turbulent years.

In retrospect, I don't know how I got the idea that he would make a U-turn and be able to help me bear my pain, when he couldn't even bear his own. But I had still hoped that he would listen and give me support.

What I didn't know at the time, among many other things I wasn't fully aware of at the time, was that you can't hope or expect another dysfunctional person to be able to help you with your own dysfunctional person. You can't expect someone to change their entire behavioral record, just like that, and suddenly live up to the fantasies, beliefs, and expectations someone else has. I made the terrible mistake of believing and expecting support from a person who absolutely could not handle conflicts or emotional events in a sensible and balanced way, and it made rejection so much more painful than it needed to be.

It wasn't my dad's fault that I had these expectations or that he couldn't live up to them, it was entirely my own fault. With hindsight, I realize that he never had the tools to handle the information and I therefore should not really have said anything to him. But now I did, and I had to live with the consequences of this decision.

Instead of comforting and providing support, my own father called me a liar. He said I was "just as disgusting as my mother", a useless traitor. I had betrayed Carl and I had betrayed my father by saying that Carl had been an oppressor. With tears in my eyes, I hung up the phone and didn't talk to him for two months. For a long time, I had been very sad and despondent about my parents' behavior during my and my siblings' upbringing. Their treatment of me as a child and the way they handled us children and how they handled their own relationship, had created very deep wounds within me.

But I wanted to forgive them. I no longer wanted to go around being angry, bitter, disappointed, hurt, or sad because they had passed on their brokenness to me and my siblings. At that time, I sought support and guidance within the church, partly because it was a cost issue and partly because I had no confidence in therapists or psychologists. This person in the church I turned to, informed me that I could write a letter each to my parents in which I addressed what hurt me the most without accusing them, and the most important thing: that I forgave them. Honestly and sincerely. I was helped to write the letters so that they were as honest, sincere, and forgiving as possible. I really wanted to forgive them, and I really didn't want to accuse them of anything. I had begun to realize that they themselves did not know much about relationships. Maybe a little too much to ask to demand something they can't give.

The letters were carefully written and carefully read to make sure the right words came through. What I didn't know then was that some people have a hard time receiving forgiveness and it was a thought that hadn't even occurred to me. It was an experience I was about to learn. In the letters, I wrote that I completely forgive them as parents for what they had done, throughout my upbringing and especially my father's statement that I would be worthless and disgusting. All the violations, all the blows, all the harsh words were forgiven, and I wrote that I would like to have them both in my life, but then they need to stop behaving so abusively and start taking responsibility for their actions. My prediction was that they would either ignore the letter and pretend nothing ever happened, as we used to do within the family, or that they would find relief and maybe even change their destructive behaviors. Should have known better, but hope is the last thing that leaves humans, it is said....

I didn't hear anything from either my father or my mother for several weeks, but still sent out an invitation to my child's naming party that they were going to have during the upcoming summer. Even though my child was nine years old at the time, they wanted to have a naming party on their naming day. Therefore, an invitation was sent out to my parents and siblings in the hope that they would come, as a kind of "peace-offering". Neither my mother nor my father got in touch. On the other hand, my siblings got in touch, but they also did not show up for the child's naming party out of pure disgust for me and my equally despicable act of forgiving our parents. But not in the way you might think.

My siblings had, within their own "parent party", been allowed to read the letters and were wonderfully upset. I was questioned what I meant by "*forgiving our parents*"? Forgave them for what? And who was I to come here with "forgiveness?" Didn't I know what a useless little piece of shit I was? Why would anyone want *my disgusting* forgiveness? The words were almost spat out via text messages and threatening phone calls from my siblings. How did I dare to *hurt* our parents like that? According to them, there was nothing that they had done wrong.

I stood as a perplexed. I didn't understand how you could be so angry and offended by being forgiven. I didn't understand how my siblings, who knew very well exactly what our parents had done and not done, how could they claim that it wasn't wrong for our parents to treat us like that? How could they consider forgiveness to be something disgusting, something perverse and despicable? Their reaction amazed me for months afterward. In the meantime, I didn't hear anything from either parent for a couple of weeks. At the end of the summer of that year, both got in touch, at different times.

My mother chose to call and immediately bring up everything that she felt that our father "exposed" her to, without the slightest thought of what she herself exposed both him and us children to. She never understood what she had done wrong, and it took a long time before she could admit that she *might* have made *some* mistakes as a parent. But just as quickly, she unfortunately slipped over to talking about herself and her experiences, as usual, and missed the chance to listen and confirm my experience. It was sad and painful, but also educational, which I will explain a little further down. Shortly after I received my mother's full account of how horrible her life had been, my father texted me that I could go to hell, that he didn't understand what he had done wrong, that he had never hurt anyone in his entire life, and that he had never hurt anyone. *Ever.*

Almost the same answer as my mother, with the difference that he used swear words and only sent text messages. I replied, as if to my mother, that he has certainly hurt people, he has hurt *me*. That he must stand for it and accept that I have felt hurt, sad, and offended, but that I loved him anyway and that he was forgiven. Just like my mother.

At that moment, I was overwhelmed by a strong anxiety, I almost panicked that my parents seemed so offended and were so angry with me. I felt a strong urge to take everything back and apologize to them for taking offense to me for the way they have raised me and my siblings. My strong conditioning to please so that my parents feel seen and loved was given free rein. Or almost free rein, with high anxiety I forced myself to hold on to my new boundaries. No more insults from the two of them.

So, I wrote three more text messages saying that he was loved, that he was allowed to be a part of my and my child's life, but he needs to stop calling me worthless and disgusting because it hurts, diminishes and is no longer okay. Enough was enough. He did not respond to any of these text messages. In sheer desperation, I called him a couple of times, he didn't answer any call.

In a panic, I wrote a couple more text messages about how loved and nice he was as a person, in a last desperate attempt to make him feel better, but I got no answer at all. I felt enormous guilt for having caused him pain. That *I* had hurt *him and my mother*. A

gain, this focus on my parents feeling good. Especially my dad. I really didn't want to be the reason he felt betrayed, unloved, or left out. It was a responsibility and a guilt I was brought up to carry early on. To be the direct cause of my parents' well-being. That everything I said or did, that could hurt them or in any way didn't confirm them in their need, was a sin and the sin could only be paid with life sentence in the form of guilt and shame. In the worst case, that one of them committed suicide. My dad never answered my text messages again. He never answered my calls or my pleas to get in touch. So, I concluded that I was no longer welcome in his life anymore and as painful as it was, I chose to honor and respect his wish to not have contact with me. That's why I didn't seek contact with him anymore.

My dad's angry text message was the last I heard from him. He died a year and a half later of cancer, I got the news the day after he passed away. By the funeral home.

Although the grief was difficult and heavy to bear at first, I consoled myself with the fact that the last thing I had written to him was that I loved him, no matter what. Friedrich Nietzsche characterizes ressentiment as the bitter envy that springs from the idea that one is wronged, and this leads to acts of revenge. Just like with everything else that my siblings felt wronged by, it was their way of dealing with the forgiveness I had written about to our parents to take revenge.

They avoided telling me about our father's cancer diagnosis, his deteriorating health, and let him believe that I didn't care. To all my questions about how he was doing and if everything was fine, they only answered briefly that it was fine. They never told me that he was dying or that he even passed away, as mentioned earlier, I got the news through the funeral home. Not even Carl, who spent time with my father and siblings frequently during this time, said anything. He had known about my father's cancer, he knew about the relationship between me and my father, and he just let it go on. I was deeply disappointed in him. That said everything about what kind of person he was. One who would rather lie and hurt to belong to a clique of individuals who also lie and hurt, than to be honest and help a parent and their adult children to reconcile. Neither of them wanted my father and I to reconcile. For my siblings it was one less to compete for attention on. After all, our family dynamic was based on competition for attention, assets, and belonging.

As for Carl, I have understood that he loves power games, gossip, and intrigue. He felt cheated and betrayed by me because I got a divorce, and he no longer had any power over me. But he could still take revenge and hurt me, by withholding information from both me and my father. It wouldn't surprise me in the least if he got sick pleasure out of this ugly game he played.

After the news of my father's death, I tried to get hold of my siblings who everyone, except Oliver and Sandra, avoided me. Sandra only answered by hateful text messages about how I would have wished for our father's death and that his death was somehow my fault. Oliver was the only one with whom it was possible to have a somewhat reasonable conversation, and he explained why they had never said anything. He explained that they were all angry and disappointed in me because our dad had told them that I hated him and that I never wanted to see him again! Our father's interpretation of my forgiveness and my demand to treat me with respect was that I hated him. Which is so incredibly tragic.

At first, it was very difficult to understand how on earth he could interpret forgiveness and boundaries as hatred and that my siblings and aunts just bought his arguments straight off. It made me angry that they seriously didn't question his reasoning or even try to make him understand, but just accepted that forgiveness and setting boundaries would be the same as hating someone. I was so put off by their unwillingness to reason and discuss, as if our father's words were facts, and so it was. It took me several weeks to get past this mental obstacle that had appeared in the form of this new information. All these people who never asked, never listened, never wanted to see any reconciliation. I asked myself how I could have been so stupid and blind and not seen this. Didn't want to see this.

During that time, I pondered upon the information, how our father chose to become bitter and hateful instead of standing up for the fact that he might not say such very nice things sometimes, especially not when he was drunk. Which was basically every day. And that my siblings and my aunts never said anything, that they never took the time to ask me what had happened between me and my father. But unfortunately, it is a culture we have within the family and within the family and that Carl appreciated, never to investigate how things really are or ask uncomfortable questions. There is a strong culture of silence and to some extent a culture of honor. You must just shut up so as not to make the family look "bad" and you should kind of just exist like that. No questions asked. Then the fact that each and every one of us has done an absolutely magnificent job of being perceived as trashy and broken, it is never talked about, and you are never allowed to hint at it.

For a while, I often wondered why this behavior is so deeply rooted in our family at both my mother's family and my father's family. There are certainly some in the families who are not as uncomfortable with asking and investigating, but of the people I know in the generations, everyone behaves basically the same. They keep quiet and agree with the one who holler the loudest or the one you take sides for and ask absolutely no probing questions.

As I said, neither did I at first. I behaved basically the same in many ways, even though I was more questioning than, for example, my siblings and parents. Despite that, I took sides and did not examine all sides of a conflict and did not always try to understand others. But as I studied spirituality and personal development and in the conversations with Martin, I have come to realize that what is outside of you - that is, how you feel, is a direct reflection of how it is on the inside, that is, how you feel and what kind of behavior you have. It also reveals what values you have and what responsibility you take for your life and what it looks like. There wasn't really much responsibility in my life before my child came into the world.

After I became a parent, I began to understand this thing about taking responsibility for everything that exists in one's life, even if it took a long time to get into as a new behavior. My earliest values were also quite skewed, because I agreed to abuse and violations as an adult. With the help of books, podcasts, YouTube clips, and psychology sessions, I slowly but surely learned that my siblings and aunts didn't and don't know any better and therefore couldn't and can't do better. My parents also didn't and don't know any better and therefore couldn't and can't do better.

What we had all been taught since childhood was that you should continue in the same old rut with destructive relationships, regardless of whether it is within the family you grew up in or other relationships you have created as an adult. You think you must put up with aggression, hatred, oppression, taunts, comments, and mockery in order to belong and get what you mistake for love. You are usually afraid of what will happen if you deviate from the ruts. You want to please and satisfy those around you so as not to be alone, left out and rejected. Dr. Phil likes to say that rejection is man's greatest fear, because we are social pack animals. He probably has a point in that. I mean, I can only look back at what I've done myself, what I've put up with, and what dysfunctional relationships I've created just to be allowed to belong to someone, to be part of a community.

CHAPTER EIGHTEEN

The time after our father's death, as I said, was difficult and insightful. When the property was divided, we siblings needed to meet and agree. It went well, everyone behaved decently, but I should have listened more to the signals I received. I was stressed and anxious about having to meet those of my siblings who had made threats and spread lies about me. The siblings who planned to kill my child in revenge for me moving away from home first. The siblings who spread mean and false rumors about me to my other siblings and our relatives. Quick, erroneous conclusions where none of them even reflected on the veracity. None of them asked me any questions and none of them listened to me as we stood in our late father's home, and I explained that I really have had nothing to do with their own dramas.

I should have suspected then and there that these siblings, even those I thought were close to me, i.e. Oliver and Sandra, were not to be trusted at all.

On paper, we siblings would help each other with the funeral, in the end Oliver, Jasmine, Amanda and Sandra made sure that neither Fredric, Arnie nor I were allowed to have any opinions. We never got information about meetings with the funeral home, we hardly even found out when or where the funeral would take place, because Jasmine, Amanda, Sandra, and Oliver didn't really want us there. Their reasoning was again that the other three of us would not have loved our father as much as they did, if at all, since all three of us had been "dismissed as children" at different times by our own father, therefore we had no "right to care" about the funeral process.

 I had no idea that Arnie or Fredric had no contact with our father either, I found out during the division of property. He had terminated contact with them too, why I don't really know. I had not had any contact with Arnie or Fredric for several years as they, just like me, have been very broken and hurt by our upbringing. I could buy that Jasmine reasoned as she did during this time, she has always had very strange and illogical reasoning. But that Oliver and Sandra behaved like that, was a bit of an unpleasant surprise. I would, unfortunately be more surprised later.

When the funeral finally took place, eight months had passed since my father's passing. The funeral was nice, but it was a bit stiff and strange meeting my paternal aunts and cousins. They were polite on site but seemed surprised that I was there. The next day I called one of my aunts because I thought that the ice was broken, maybe we can recreate our previous relationship? We couldn't.

My aunt was very cold and dismissive and was not the least bit interested in talking to me. That's when I realized that my child and I are completely excluded from the family. It was then that I realized that these relatives that I had spent time with, played with and previously considered to have had a good relationship with, had never had any warmer feelings for me or my child. They didn't want to have anything to do with me and they didn't want to know how I've been doing. I wrote a letter to my relatives, explaining everything regarding the fallout from my father, from my perspective just so they have both sides of the story. I thanked them for everything they have done during my childhood and then said goodbye to them. I'm not going to force myself into their lives and I don't want people in my life who doesn't want to be there. We are better off without each other.

Just a few weeks after our father's funeral, my sister Sandra unfortunately committed suicide. She couldn't cope with life anymore. Although it came as a shock, it was a bit expected. She had never felt good mentally and had attempted suicide more times than I can keep track of. It was only a matter of time before she would succeed, no matter how much the rest of us tried to prevent her from dying. Even if we siblings didn't get along, each of us at least took care of Sandra in her very bad mental state. Despite our wounded relationships, we looked after her. Despite all the hatred from her, I looked after her. Loved her.

I don't know exactly what the relationship was like between my siblings and Sandra, but between her and me there were many times eternal conversations to try to get her to live, to find healing and joy. Several calls from psychiatry's emergency department about admissions and just as many calls about threats and self-harm. Her life was chaotic and intense. Which led to the rest of us around her, also having to live a forced chaotic and intense life based on how she felt for the day. For the moment. She could be very happy in the morning and never want to stop talking, only to have tried to kill herself in the evening and then not want to talk to you for weeks. It took an enormous amount of time and energy to spend time with her and I admit that I didn't always have the energy to do it. It was stressful and hard.

She was always in a very bad mental state, and unfortunately, she didn't get the right help from the public health care. To some extent, she also didn't want help or accept help. In her world, there was nothing that worked or was right. Everything was wrong and it was everyone else's fault. She could not and did not want to take responsibility for her own well-being or to make other, healthier decisions. In retrospect, I understand that she, just like our mother, probably suffered very badly from Borderline Disorder and she had many, very severe traumas behind her, much more difficult than mine and my siblings combined, and no conditions to deal with it. But she was an adult, she had the right to say no to care, help and support, which she did. In my eyes, she should have been involuntarily admitted and treated. But would it have changed the outcome or just prolonged her suffering further? I don't know. The only thing I know is that she suffered so much and there was nothing I could do about it. No one else either.

When the news came that Sandra had died, I sat unknowingly just a hundred meters from the hospital where she ended up. I sat in a meeting with a doctor regarding my child and had my mobile phone turned off. When I left the meeting and turned on my phone, I had several missed calls from Jasmine and Oliver, my mother, and my grandmother. I understood that something was wrong. I called Jasmine, who replied that Sandra was dead. That she had successfully killed herself that very same morning. Even though I could go the few steps to the hospital and go to the others and say goodbye to Sandra, I chose to go home. I was in shock, and I didn't want to see my beloved sister dead. It wasn't a memory I wanted to carry with me. I didn't want to stand there with my siblings who I barely knew and say goodbye to what until now, had been my sister that I was supposed to call during the day. I didn't get the equation together in my head there and then. It was too much.

I informed my job of what had happened and was on sick leave for three weeks. I called Elin and told her and finally I needed to go home and sit with my child and tell them that their only reasonably present aunt, was now dead. We were all in grief and shock, both my child and I, my siblings, my mother, and grandmother. When the property was divided, only Arnie, Jasmine and I could be present with our mother. It was hard to have to go through my sister's things, choose what to throw away, what to give away. Choosing what we who were there thought the other siblings wanted.

The same friend who helped my child and me escape from Gunnar, looked after my child in the meantime. They couldn't bear to go through their aunt's things.

The funeral was held a couple of weeks later, in the same church as our father, in the community where we all grew up as children. Also here, Jasmine, Amanda and Oliver tried to stop me, Arnie, Fredric, and our mother from coming. They didn't think we were as close to Sandra as they were, just because we lived in other cities and because of our childhood. They were cruel and blamed us for Sandra's death. That we didn't do enough or that we didn't care enough about her. I understand that they too were in grief and shock, but to behave like that, is undignified. None of us were to blame for her death. It was a choice she made and had made so many times before.

These siblings temporarily stopped their hate campaigns and allowed those who wanted to come to the funeral, to go to the funeral. Gunnar was unfortunately one of these who came. He, just like Carl, had continued to have close contact with my siblings after my child and I had left. Why he spent time with my siblings and what he got out of it all, I don't know. They are all adults and do what they want, but I find it strange that a sixty-year-old man hangs out with people under the age of thirty, who also happen to be closely related to the person he thought "destroyed his home". What my siblings got out of it; I don't know either. I can't be bothered anymore. I ignored Gunnar and his children and have not spoken to him since I left him. Elin came along as support, as the good friend that she is, but we didn't stay at any gathering after the funeral. I couldn't bear to sit there and talk about my sister, who I barely even realized was dead.

The weeks and months afterwards were a bit like a fog, every day I was about to call or text Sandra only to realize that she wouldn't be there to answer. I checked my phone several times, hoping that she would have sent a funny text message, as she did sometimes. There were no more text messages. There is a saying about "getting over the grief", but it is not something you can get over. The grief and loss will always be there. You just learn to live with it. Even though I would most like to be able to back the band, save my sister and keep her, I also realize that she didn't want to stay. We talked a lot about it, she, and I, that even though it hurts me, I must accept that she didn't live a good life. It would be so incredibly selfish of me to want her to stay, let her live. She suffered so terribly and why should she continue such a life for the rest of us? Why should our egos, fears, and beliefs about how things should be, force her to continue living a life she was miserable about? She did not deserve her suffering, nor could she get out of it in any other way. I accept it now.

Just as I accept that life is less chaotic and intense now that she has ended her suffering. At first, I was ashamed of these feelings, but the truth is that life for my child and me is much calmer and peaceful now. All these abrupt throws and hasty commitments call about Sandra's well-being. Suddenly, we could relax in a different way, although I sincerely wish we had been able to do it with Sandra still alive.

I don't advocate suicide as a solution to mental problems, but I have been suicidal myself, I know what the thinking is like. And I know that in this case, Sandra is better off now than she ever was in all her years here on earth. She is still loved by me, my child and by our other relatives. I still find things I'd like to tell her, just to realize, that she is probably already laughing about it all in her heaven. She is no longer here physically, but she is always with us in our hearts.

CHAPTER NINETEEN

During these eight months before Sandra's death and funeral, I had a fairly good contact with Paulina. As mentioned before, we had resumed contact a few years earlier, after a couple of years of occasional contact. Not because we didn't want to talk, as I thought anyway, but because we simply let time pass, as many unfortunately do. During this time, Paulina was unusually inquisitive and wanted to socialize. However, always at her place.

Even though she, unlike me, had access to a car and was often in the city I lived in, her demand was always that I go to her home. I invited her to my home several times, but she never came to my place, I was the one who had to go the three metric miles by bus to her home if we were to meet at all. I should have listened to the red flags again, but again I was so busy maintaining what little contact I had that I ignored what was obviously skewed in our relationship.

Once at her place or when we talked on the phone, she very much wanted to talk about my relationships with Carl and with Gunnar. She wanted to know "everything" about my child's development and autism, and even questioned me about things in my childhood. There and then, I thought that she seemed unusually curious, but attributed it to the fact that we had a lot to "catch up". However, there came a day when I found out otherwise. That day came on the same day my sister died.

In addition to the fact that I had planned to call Sandra on that tragic day, I was also going to call Paulina. But for understandable reasons, I couldn't do this. I texted Paulina and explained what had happened and that I would not call her as we had decided earlier. I couldn't cope, I wanted to be by myself and take in that my beloved sister was dead. However, Paulina did not listen to this, and called a moment later. I didn't answer, I just went home and cried. I wrote back to Paulina to apologize, said I really didn't have the energy to talk to her, I'd call when I felt that I had the energy. She called again, whereupon I repeated that I really didn't have the energy to talk to her or anyone else for that matter right then and there.

After about a week, I felt that I might have the energy to talk to Paulina. I called her, but she didn't answer. I sent a text message and suggested a time she could call back if she wanted. She never called back and didn't send a text message. Weeks passed, and in the mess with my siblings, funeral, and further division of property, I unexpectedly received information that Paulina had used me and my family as entertainment for her friends. It was friends she made when Carl groomed me as a teenager and Paulina thought I was disgusting to be with an older man and chose to end our relationship because of it.

I honestly do not know if the information below is completely true. Since this came out, I have not been able to get hold of Paulina. She hasn't responded to texts, calls, or letters, so I haven't been able to ask her if it's true. Which is an indication that something in the relationship between her and me is not genuine. What do indicate that the claims are true, is that the informant had information that they reasonably should not have, because I have never talked to them before. This is information only Paulina has had access to through our meetings and conversations.

So, what I found out was that Paulina has told these new friends of hers about my family, our upbringing and all the "blunders" I have done throughout my life. As a child and as well as an adult. She has talked about how disgusting Carl was, how disgusting I was to enter into a relationship with him, as well as the relationship with Gunnar. She has talked about my father's death and now my sister's suicide. The only reason she had asked all these questions and kept in touch during this time, was to have more sloppy details to share. More to laugh at, more to rejoice in her childhood friend's traumas, mistakes, and family tragedies. Despite the new information, I invited her to my sister's funeral, partly because she had grown up with me, as my friend, and knew who my sister was. Partly because it was a chance to meet and maybe talk it out, after all, Paulina lived only ten minutes' walking distance from the church where the funeral took place.

She never came. She also never responded to my invitation.

I stopped trying to get hold of Paulina after that. It landed inside me there and then that I have most likely only been one big clown in her life. Something broke in me when the realization finally fell into place; me, my family, and our lives; has only been an amusement park for some. We have been someone's spectacle, circus, someone to make fun of. And I realized that if Paulina really wanted to give me a different version, a different truth than the one I had been given, she would have gotten in touch. It has now been over three years, and she still hasn't heard from her. So, I bury that relationship as well. Just as I symbolically bury my siblings

I never reconnected with Amanda, after our father's division of property and funeral. She is too manipulative and unreliable. Our grandmother called me unexpectedly one day and was very upset. It had turned out that Amanda, who had lived for free for several months with our grandmother, together with her two children while waiting for an apartment through social services (which she also feels persecuted by), stole five thousand bucks from our grandmother. She left her home in a mess as soon as she gained access to the new apartment.

Right after the move, Amanda started writing a lot of hateful messages to our grandmother and our mother and then posted these messages on social media for everyone to read. Just like she did with me. When my grandmother told me this, I was actually glad. Not because my grandmother has been exploited, but because she and others finally understood what Amanda does to people.

I explained that this is exactly what Amanda did to me so many years ago and it was nice that those who unreflectively believed in Amanda then, now got to taste this experience themselves and realize that she is not who she claims to be. My grandmother surprisingly apologized. She didn't have had to apologize, because even if she has made her mistakes, I believe that you can never demand or expect an apology from anyone. But it still felt nice that for once she was humble and kind for once.

As for my other remaining siblings, Sandra's death has led to the end of many different things. Jasmine and Oliver can't talk about anything other than the day our sister died. They dwell on her life, as well as their own lives over and over again, stuck in the past and in all the pain. Yes, we have had a painful childhood and our sister's death is tragic. Her life was tragic, but that doesn't mean we should stop looking ahead and stop living. We need to accept and respect her choice to end her life, just as we need to accept that our lives have been dysfunctional and difficult.

It is not the same as justifying everything that has happened, it is not the same as liking what has been. But it is the same as taking responsibility for one's own part in the suffering and making peace with all the wounded, wounded, and broken.

Oliver is no longer the brother I knew as a child and young adult. After all the betrayals and lies on his part, I have realized that I have been very naïve and gullible. I have chosen to believe his words before; I chose to believe only good things about him. I thought I knew him, but honestly, I never knew him at all. I only knew him as much as my own blinders allowed.

He might come back, but I don't think so. Unfortunately, I think that just like with our father, bitterness and hatred takes over and will rule his life until the end. I mourn the brother I thought I had. I mourn the relationship and community that I saw in my blindness, but which was never there except in my perception.

Jasmine and I have never been close, not even as children. She has never liked me and never liked my child. Nowadays I'm okay with that. She doesn't have to like us. The only thing I ask of her is to just not hurt us. I can seldomly visit her, because there is a risk that she will resume her plan to stab my child or maybe me.

She sends nice text messages sometimes; I answer them politely. I think that, unlike Amanda and Oliver, a part of her wants to have a relationship with me, just like a part of me wants to have a relationship with her, but

that neither she nor I know what that relationship
should look like.

Without support and outside help in the form of a
family therapist, I don't think we will get very far. Our
upbringing and all the different experiences have
become an ocean of wounds and mistrust that we
cannot overcome ourselves. I work actively to forgive
both myself and her for everything we have and have
not done. As well as accepting that we will probably
die in our different worlds and if that is what the
Universe has planned, then so be it.

I don't have any further contact with Arnie either,
despite several attempts. Just like with Jasmine, there is
a desire from both of us to have some kind of
relationship, but without outside help, we don't have
much chance of building a stable relationship. As a
person, Arnie is very evasive and does not like to take
responsibility for his life or to talk to people who
disagree with him or who challenge his perceptions of
how things are and have been. He too is stuck in the
past and can mostly only talk about the violence we
experienced as children, the violence our mother

experienced in the relationship with our father and Sandra's death. Because I want to talk about other things, talk about new things and explore other perspectives and often challenge Arnie in his perceptions, I understand that he finds it difficult to talk to me and thus avoids it completely. Today I understand that it's not personal, really. We're just not in the same place and just like with Jasmine and Oliver, I've accepted that we'll probably continue to live in different worlds until we die and that's okay. It's sad, but okay.

Fredric lives far from another place and enjoys only having contact via text message. He is surprisingly the one of my siblings I have got good contact with after everything that has happened. We had no contact for several years, as Sandra and Jasmine in particular, had spread lies about him to me, and about me to him. Which resulted in us not wanting to talk to each other because we didn't reflect more deeply on what we were told. After Sandra's death, I asked him some questions about what's been said and done, and we realized that everything said to us, by our other siblings, was not true at all. That everything has been a lie, created to hold on to the divisions and friction between us. A way to maintain the status quo for those who benefited from it, i.e., Sandra, Amanda, and Jasmine. Oliver, for his own personal reasons, does not want to have anything to do with Fredric. Arnie and Fredric, on the other hand, are close and hopefully find comfort in each other as brothers. Or I hope that's the way it is anyway. Fredric and I exchanged numbers at Sandra's funeral and have kept in touch ever since.

My mother, she still has a very hard time talking about anything other than herself. I know this now. We don't have a great relationship, but she has stated that she wants to try to create a better relationship. She goes to behavioral therapy and even though it is difficult for her, she now tries to understand me, and I try to understand her. I also work actively to not continue to accuse her of things in the past. I need to see her for who she is and not the mother I think she should have been. She will never be anyone else and why should I continue to be angry and bitter about something she can't change? We don't always agree on things, and that's okay. She doesn't have to agree with me about certain experiences and I don't have to agree with her. We can coexist anyway. Without hatred, without threats and without insults.

My grandmother, who is now very old, has also started to get in touch a little more. Just like with my mother, I try to meet her where she is and not where I think she should be. And to meet her without accusations and hurtful words. We don't need more of that in our lives. It's time to let go of what has been and forgive both others and me for my own participation in all of this.

CHAPTER TWENTY

At the time of writing, my child and I are looking for exciting new challenges and new joyful experiences. We are free to create the lives we want to live, no one controlling us or limiting us. No one belittling us or making us feel wrong for being who we are. For a long time, my life was lined with dysfunctional behaviors that I slowly but surely had to process and change. Yes, many people have let me down, made me angry, sad, despairing, and created feelings of enormous alienation and depression.

But these people have done so because I have allowed it on some level, just as they have allowed me on some level to hurt them. My search for community and belonging led to many bad and not very well thought out decisions. This led to more suffering, anxiety, and a constant search to be accepted. As a direct result of a dysfunctional childhood, my personal integrity was blown away. For most of my life, I owned no boundaries. I was everyone else's property and everyone else's toy and it's not something I want to pass on to my child.

Today I have strong boundaries and have begun to feel my own personal integrity. I have chosen to live single, partly because I do not yet trust other people enough to let them into my life, and partly because I do not fully trust my own judgment when it comes to other people. I have demonstrably not had a good judgment before. In addition, I don't feel the need to enter any intimate or romantic relationship with others. I've gotten a taste of the freedom to do what I want, talk to whoever I want, dress how I want and identify how I want. For those who have previously lived in various forms of captivity, either through political or social roles, control in the home or locked by their previous behaviors, the new freedom is so valuable that one does not want to expose it to any risks. If my and my child's individual freedom is at risk of being compromised in a relationship, then I let that relationship die by itself. No romantic relationship is worth that price.

Nowadays I allow myself more and more to be just as autistic as I am, which means that I accept that I am introverted, creative, odd, and self-committed. I'm more open about the fact that I don't do well in large social contexts, that I don't eat certain types of dishes or mix certain types of food. I more often speak up if there is too much social interaction or if there is something neuro normative, I do not understand.

I still mask my way of functioning in some situations, but I'm better at reflecting on when it happens and why I do it. I allow myself to be different, to be Sami and Swedish Finns, to not follow the norm or understand the Swedish society that I have never felt a part of. I no longer need to be accepted or liked by others. Others are allowed to have their opinions and thoughts about me and my child, it is not my business. Today, I understand that it is never personally directed at us, even though it may look like it. It's just a reflection of the other person's dysfunctionality, the other person's brokenness, and limitations.

Through my experiences and learnings, I teach my child that we must take responsibility for our actions and their consequences, even the less pleasant ones, and that sometimes you must move on and leave some people along the way. Even if it feels difficult and painful, we cannot force anyone to go down the same path as us. We cannot force others to change or make different decisions in their lives. We also cannot stay in a place that is not good or welcoming to us. Some people follow us just a little bit on the way, the rest we must keep walking without them. We will meet new people during the walk, we will leave some and embrace others. We will be hurt by others in the future as well, just as we will hurt others. That's what life is like. You can't be everyone's best friend, nor should you be everyone's best friend, whether it's an outsider or a close relative.

However, you should always be your own best friend, and stay respectful to those you meet, while at the same time being sensitive to the signals you receive. It is important to pay attention if something feels wrong and if someone starts to take up areas of your life that you do not really want to give up or feel comfortable with. Then it's time to put your foot down. If you get hostility back, then choose to go another way.

You are not obliged to stay in an unhealthy relationship or environment. You are not obliged to take responsibility for the behavior of others, and you are not obliged to accept bad treatment, no matter how a person justifies it. I have learned that you must let others live their lives the way they want to live it, even if you do not agree with their behaviors or life choices. I've learned that everyone has their own paths to tread, their own life stories to learn from, and that's okay, even if it means you are by yourself on your own path.

I would like to conclude with a few words from Jay Shetty, a person whose wisdom is very great, despite his small age:

If you focus on the past, you're controlled by fear. If you're focused on the future, you're controlled by anxiety. If you focus on others, you are controlled by them.

If you focus on yourself, you live in peace. Jay Shetty

All the best

-    Annie